Quantum God, Fractal Jesus

How Isaac Newton Redefined God Without Really Meaning to,
And Why We Really Don't Get God

Andrew Fletcher

Quantum God, Fractal Jesus

How Isaac Newton Redefined God Without Really Meaning to,
And Why We Really Don't Get God

Andrew Fletcher

Copyright © 2010 by Andrew Fletcher

Second Edition Copyright © 2012 by Andrew Fletcher

All rights reserved. No part of this book may be reproduced in any form or by any electronic or mechanical means, including information storage and retrieval systems, without permission in writing from the publisher, except by a reviewer, who may quote brief passages in a review.

Published by fletchpub at Lulu

ISBN: 978-0-578-06550-2

Set in 11 point Garamond type

The science in this book is used in a series of seminars developed and given worldwide by LUE, Inc. For information on hosting the seminars, to see the bibliography from which the seminars were developed, to see a list of places where the seminars have been given, to buy the seminars in book or DVD form, or for a history of the seminars and the organization, please visit www.lifeuniverseverything.org.

Life, the Universe, and Everything, Inc.

Also known as TOK Seminars

c/o TOK Seminars, PO Box 62627,

Colorado Springs CO 80920 USA

+1.719.660.2602

Table of Contents

Page	Chapter	Title
9		Preface
13		Introduction
23	One	Aristotle, Newton, and Why Pretty Darn Good is Not Perfect
31	Two	The More-Than-Infinite God
39	Three	Nothing is Really Something, and Vice Versa
47	Four	Quantum God
55	Five	Quantum God in Two Chapters at the Same Time
67	Six	Good Parking Spots, Hot Wives, and Great Hair
75	Seven	Chaos out of Order
83	Eight	Our God is an Awesomely Chaotic God
91	Nine	Holy, Holy, Wholly Complex God
99	Ten	The Gentle Whisper of Math
107	Eleven	Fractalated Universe
117	Twelve	Fractal Jesus
127	Thirteen	It's God Time
135	Fourteen	Order out of Chaos
145	Fifteen	The Meaning of Life
155	Sixteen	Lucy, You Got Some 'Splainin' To Do
165	Seventeen	It's All God's Fault. OK, Not Really.
175	Conclusion:	The End
181	Extra Bits	Free will, knowing it all, evolution

"Usually, even a non-Christian knows something about the earth, the heavens, and the other elements of this world, about the motion and orbit of the stars and even their size and relative positions, about the predictable eclipses of the sun and moon, the cycles of the years and the seasons, about the kinds of animals, shrubs, stones, and so forth, and this knowledge he holds to as being certain from reason and experience. Now, it is a disgraceful and dangerous thing for an infidel to hear a Christian, presumably giving the meaning of Holy Scripture, talking nonsense on these topics; and we should take all means to prevent such an embarrassing situation, in which people show up vast ignorance in a Christian and laugh it to scorn. The shame is not so much that an ignorant individual is derided, but that people outside the household of the faith think our sacred writers held such opinions, and, to the great loss of those for whose salvation we toil, the writers of our Scripture are criticized and rejected as unlearned men. If they find a Christian mistaken in a field which they themselves know well and hear him maintaining his foolish opinions about our books, how are they going to believe those books in matters concerning the resurrection of the dead, the hope of eternal life, and the kingdom of heaven, when they think their pages are full of falsehoods on facts which they themselves have learnt from experience and the light of reason?"

(Augustine of Hippo, 354-430 AD; The Literal Meaning of Genesis, vol. 1, ch.19.)

Preface

A few years ago, I wrote a book called *Life, the Universe, and Everything* that has since sold literally dozens of copies, not only to my mother, but to as many as several of my friends and to others to whom I really just gave a copy, which doesn't exactly count as "selling" *per se* except that somebody actually bought them. OK, that would have been me, but, as we shall see, I count for something in the grand scheme of things.

I do remember one young lady to whom I tossed a copy of the book and the look on her face, a priceless look, one that all authors look forward with great anticipation to seeing, a look that can only be described as "Why are you giving me this and what am I supposed to do with it?" I had the same look when my children were born and the nurse handed me this lumpy bit of my own personal DNA in human form. No, really, that was not true with my own kids, but I have to confess that it was totally true with anybody else's kids that happened to get handed to me as though I was receiving a Great Treasure, when, as a man, I had the feeling that I was being given a ticking bomb of potential, well, you know, stuff that comes out of other people's children when you are holding them pretending to be thrilled.

Anyway, I wrote this other book first, and it would be really good for you to go read it before you read this. It's not essential, but it would help. I'm trying to find a middle ground here that will cause you to go buy the other book first, read it, and then read this one, but without scaring you away from reading this one without having read the other one. How'm I doing so far?

There's a really good reason for you to go read it: it explains a lot of things that I'm not going to explain quite so thoroughly this time around, things that at first don't make much sense, and then as you spend a lot of time thinking about them, make even less sense, until finally you have exhausted the entire capacity of your brain only to discover that they not only don't make sense to you, they don't make sense to anybody, and yet they represent the fundamentals of science and the way that the universe is put together. So I guess that when I said "explains a lot of things" a minute ago, that was something of an exaggeration.

There's something else. I wrote the other book for two groups of people in particular, along with anyone else who wanted to read it, but most people fit into one of these two groups. The first group was and is those people who once believed that science is pretty straightforward and easy enough for smart people to understand if they spend enough time at it. That group found out how wrong they were about that. This is also the group that believes that science has explained away any need for any sort of god or God or gods, explained it away finally and completely. For them, God is dead. God remains dead. God was always dead, at least in the sense that he didn't exist in the first place. ("Dead" is not really a good term to describe that, but we'll let that go.)

What this group learned about science and God is that, as it turned out, it is perfectly possible to be massively intelligent and still believe in God on the basis of the science alone. You aren't *compelled* to believe in God because of the science, but you can make a rational, reasonable choice to believe in God, just as you can make a rational, reasonable choice to disbelieve in any god at all. You can also believe or disbelieve in God or gods for stupid, irrational reasons. It may not ultimately be a matter of intelligence, but rather of choice based on evidence, evidence which is the same for everyone, but which everyone interprets in his or her own way to support whatever choice he or she has decided to make with respect to deity.

The other group was and is those people who are religious, who feel both threatened and exhilarated by science when it comes to God, who may feel that it is hard (verging on impossible) to have both faith and intelligence, to believe in both God and science in the same brain at the same time, and who crave in their hearts of hearts to integrate both brains and heart, mind and soul, to be able to be intelligent believers.

As a sidelight, it was also for religious people who think that science is completely wrong about origins and that their own particular book of theology has the right story, even if science says that it's hokum. What they had the opportunity to learn, and the choice to do so, was that the universe is vastly more interesting and intriguing than they ever could have imagined, and by extension, so was, and is, God.

Which brings us, finally, to this book. I'm not really sure who this book is for, so feel free to read it regardless of what you think. But the purpose of this book is to re-examine the assumptions that we talked about in the first book about the way the universe is put together. In *Life, the Universe and Everything*, we noted that scientists had made some assumptions about the structure of nature back in the 1600s that needed to go away, but haven't yet. In this book, we are going to see if religious people have done exactly the same thing. That is, we are going to present the proposal that people of faith have taken the 400-year-old flawed or flat-out wrong assumptions from science about the structure of the universe and applied those assumptions to what they think they understand about God and their faith, coming up with a flawed and/or flat-out wrong understanding of God.

As an interesting by-product, we may discover that people of science who have rejected the idea of God or deity have rejected the wrong God, a God defined by presuppositions that no longer hold true with respect to science and faith together. People who reject the idea of God do so for a variety of reasons, not all of which are we going to deal with. Some reject God because they don't like the God they don't believe in. There's too much pointless suffering in the world, for example, and they refuse to believe in a God who seems blithely to allow, cause and/or encourage the suffering. Others reject God because of the fanaticism, cruelty, banality, intolerance, and pedantry of religious people, or, in a related sort of way, because of the often hideous nature of the history of religious peoples as they slaughter each other over arcane differences over dogma or slaughter nonbelievers because they are nonbelievers. Some reject God because he seems to call his various peoples to do these terrible things to each other inside the faiths and others outside or in differing faiths. Many reject God these days because, as we said above, believing in any God without any evidence is for stupid people, and nobody wants to be stupid.

More specifically, they reject the supernatural God, the God who works miracles, because miracles are thought to be unscientific. Interestingly, many believers believe only in a supernatural God, a God who works only via miracles and not really in a natural way very often or significantly. It is a conundrum, one that does not seem to have a solution with feet in both science and religion. We shall see.

We each have presuppositions, assumptions we make about life and nature, and we tend to operate under those presuppositions without challenging them in any conscious way, or, in fact, by being conscious of them at all. We let our senses and our ability to observe the world around us define that world, thereby assuming that this world is as it seems to be. It is made of matter and rules, solid stuff and gassy stuff and liquidy stuff, and rules like gravity and electricity. We theoretically can understand it in its totality. It is rational and reasonable, comprehensible and definable, ultimately describable and predictable in all of its parts. Those of us who are people of faith have a similar viewpoint toward that faith.

On both sides, mystery leaves us uncomfortable, and I know as I write that that people of science will say in strong terms, Not True!, Mystery challenges us to investigate deeper and better, and people of faith will say, Not True!, There is a mystery to faith that gives it power, and to both I will say that these things are true in the abstract, but when I confront you, as I will, with mysteries in the specific, as I did in *Life, the Universe, and Everything* and as I will in this book, you may not be so sanguine, so pleased to meet those mysteries. Mysteries that fit neatly within our paradigms are just fine; it is the mysteries that threaten the paradigms that are both the most important and the least pleasant.

And thus, it is those mysteries we will explore together. We may not find answers we like, but we will encounter the questions that all of us have. I'm not sure I like the answers, but I do have the same questions that all of us seem to have.

The two most surprising ideas in Plato's hidden philosophy may be explained simply. First, the musical and mathematical structures he hid in his writings show that he was committed to the radical idea that the universe is controlled not by the gods on Olympus but by mathematical and scientific law. Today we take it for granted that the book of nature is written in the language of mathematics, but it was a dangerous and heretical idea when it struggled for acceptance in the Scientific Revolution of the 1600s. Giordano Bruno was burnt at the stake and Galileo was condemned and imprisoned. After Socrates was executed for sowing doubts about Greek religion, Plato had every reason to hide his commitment to a scientific view of the cosmos. But we now know that Plato anticipated the key idea of the Scientific Revolution by some 2000 years.

Perhaps even more surprisingly, Plato's positive philosophy shows us how to combine science and religion. Today we hear much of the culture wars between believers and atheists, between those who insist our world is imbued with meaning and value and those who argue for materialism and evolution. For Plato, music was mathematical and mathematics was musical. In particular, we hear musical notes harmonising with each other when their pitches form simple ratios. For him, the perception of this beauty in music was at once the perception of a beauty inherent in mathematics. Thus mathematics and the laws governing our universe were imbued with beauty and value: they were divine. Modern scientists don't ask where their fundamental laws come from; for Plato, the beauty and order inherent in mathematical law meant its source was divine (a Pythagorean version of modern deism). Plato may light a middle way through today's culture wars.

(New Research on Plato and Pythagoras, Dr. Jay Kennedy, University of Manchester, http://personalpages.manchester.ac.uk/staff/jay.kennedy)

(Plato: 428/427 BC – 348/347 BC)

Introduction

At the time of this writing in summer of 2008, the tension between science and religion is high and shows no signs of going away. The New Atheists, among them such intellectual luminaries as Richard Dawkins (the high priest of atheism, author of *The God Delusion*), Sam Harris (*The End of Faith* and *Letters to a Christian Nation*), Christopher Hitchens (*God is not Great*) and Daniel Dennett (*Breaking the spell: Religion as a Natural Phenomenon*) have been well received and widely read as they have mounted an assault on religion in the world today.

People of faith have fought back but by and large are losing the PR battle despite some learned and considered responses. Atheists are almost gleeful, feeling as though they have dealt religion a deathblow as far as the intellect is concern. There is a strong sense that the war for the mind has been won by the new atheism.

My sense is that the religion is not going away any time soon, and that the intellectuals of the faith are able to convince many of the faithful that their beliefs are intellectually legitimate, but they are not winning many converts from the other side. My sense is also and however that the other side is winning converts to atheism, particularly among the best and the brightest of high school and university students around the world. Numbers to validate that sense will be hard to come by, so we'll just have to take it on faith. So to speak.

The focal point of the debate/hostilities is clearly evolution* and creationism*, the latter of which includes a number of flavors: young earth creationism*, old earth creationism*, and Intelligent Design* as the most significant. They are most often lumped together in the popular press and thus in the mind of the public, though there are distinct and important differences, which we may get into later.

The thought by the New Atheists is that young earth creationism, which insists upon a literal interpretation of Biblical creation (miraculous creation by fiat, not by natural processes), is monumentally primitive and superstitious, the province of small and fearful minds, the birthplace of intolerance and ignorance.

In a talk I gave to a small group of students in Singapore many years ago, a young man, a Hong Kong Chinese boy named Albert, went to great pains to try to convince me that the Bible mandated a six-day, 6000-year creation cosmology. His argument was that "if you can't believe what Genesis says," then you open the door to disbelief in Christianity in all of its parts, especially disbelief in Christ himself.

Albert was a firm atheist. His point, the same position taken by the New Atheists, is that any religion ignorant enough to teach a six-day, 6000-year cosmology is ignorant in its totality, and the essential claims of that faith (the birth, life, death and resurrection of Jesus) are no better than belief in unicorns or leprechauns.

Thus a hierarchy of assumptions by the New Atheists—there is no evidence of the existence of God, all the evidence of science points toward a completely natural process that produced the universe and ultimately life within it, anyone who denies that evidence is being willfully ignorant and superstitious, all faith is superstition, benign at best, but much more often malignantly intolerant and potentially vicious, and hence religion and religious people are harmful to the planet and the life thereon. Belief in God is not reasonable, religion is not reasonable, and religious people are not reasonable.

Though there have been many well-reasoned responses from people of faith, the sad truth is that most of those refuse to acknowledge fully the damage that religion and religious people have actually done to humanity and to the planet over the centuries, instead trying to minimize or justify the horrors that we have perpetrated. However, it is not our purpose to follow that path. We have another direction entirely to pursue.

The history of religion and science together is fascinating to look at. Science didn't really exist for most of human history, so religion in its various forms provided the explanations of natural phenomena that man required, explanations that were not always, uh, especially accurate. These explanations masqueraded as science, without using the word "science," of course, since the word "science" as it now refers to the study of the natural universe around us did not really become common until the 19th Century—the word "scientist" was first used in 1833.

The study of the natural world apart from religious explanations is ancient and can be investigated on your own. What is germane to our purposes is both how right we sometimes were in formulating explanations, and more importantly, how wrong we often were. For instance, Plato and Aristotle were fascinatingly correct in some of their observations, tragically wrong in others, though understandably so given the limitations of their abilities to make observations.

We might also note that modern scientists suffer the same fate. Einstein changed human history with his discoveries, but spent his life chasing a Theory of Everything* to which he was denied because the technology did not yet exist to tell him what he needed to know in order to go further, and he was critically wrong in his rejection of both Big Bang* and Quantum Mechanics*. The same is true at this very moment with respect to String Theory*, Loop Quantum Gravity*, Inflation*, the Multi-verse*, the Cyclic Universe*, the Ekpyrotic Universe*, Hawkings' Flexiverse*, the Self-organizing universe*, and many others: we simply don't have the technology to be able to provide any *direct* evidence at all that these might be viable as theories, and we may never have the technology to do so. As quantum physicist Wolfgang Pauli once remarked, "That's not right. It's not even wrong." Without any evidence one way or the other, we can't even say that they are wrong.

By the end of the 19th Century, scientists had attained what one might call a predictable level of arrogance. Human reason was thought to reign supreme, sure to reveal the great secrets of nature, the universe itself melting under our intellectual assault. Newton, the demigod of physics and indeed of science, had shown the world that the universe could be described in simple, elegant equations. Maxwell's equations revealed electromagnetism, Darwin's theory showed biological change (though as yet without a motor to drive it), Kepler, Copernicus and Galileo had redefined and restructured our understanding of the universe and earth's place within it, and the 19th Century list of those who formed the world's first scientific community, along with their discoveries, is stunning: Pasteur, Edison, Faraday, Bell, Curie, Doppler, Foucault, Gauss, Hertz, Lord Kelvin, Mendel, Nobel, Tessla, Freud, and the list goes on. That naïve arrogance and childlike belief in the wonders of human reason drew forth predictions that today would be considered laughable, and are, but for similar sentiments that continue to issue forth from today's thinkers. For example:

In 1888, Simon Newcomb, an American astronomer, concluded that, "We are probably nearing the limit of all we can know about astronomy." In 1888 and up until 1929, all we knew about the universe was that there was one galaxy (and we didn't know that it was a galaxy), with 6,188 stars listed in catalogues in the year 1888. We now estimate that there are 140 *billion* galaxies outside of the estimated 100 to 400 *billion* stars in our own galaxy, literally more stars in the universe than there are grains of sand on the earth.[1]

Albert Michelson said in 1894 that "The more important fundamental laws and facts of physical science have all been discovered, and…the possibility of their being supplanted in consequence of new discoveries is exceedingly remote." And none other than Lord Kelvin said in 1900 that "There is nothing new to be discovered in physics now. All that remains is more and more precise measurement."

It was in 1900 that Max Planck started the Quantum revolution that made mockery of both Michelson and Kelvin; in 1905 Einstein continued that revolution with his discovery of the photoelectric effect and then started one of his own with Special Relativity*, followed in 1915 by one of the greatest upsets and discoveries in human history, General Relativity*. Both Quantum Mechanics and the two Theories of Relativity essentially destroyed our classic notions of the structure of the universe and all that is within it in ways that the

---

[1] http://astronomy.swin.edu.au/~gmackie/billions.html; **To see the Universe in a Grain of Taranaki Sand,** Glen Mackie, *[appeared in North and South magazine, May, 1999]*

vast majority of today's educated and informed humanity is unaware of, completely rewriting the science of the universe.

Many have justifiably laughed and scoffed at religion's refusal to accept new scientific discoveries that seemed to challenge the way that the universe was put together. The Church struggled with Copernicus and then Galileo, among others, over what has been called the Geocentric and perhaps Anthrocentric views of the universe, that is, that the perfect creation of God placed earth at the center of the universe and man at the center of that. In time, religion recovered and all of mankind with it (apart from the Flat Earth Society[2]) and we now recognize that it is not necessary for the earth to be either flat or at the center of the universe for God to exist.

In light of the (now known to be) ridiculous claims by the world's finest scientists at the end of the 19th Century that science was essentially finished, one can justify a certain amount of skepticism with respect to the declarations of well-meaning scientists, who make their claims on the basis of the evidence available to them at the time. Whereas religion is criticized for making absolutist claims, science often does the same, and offers no apology when the claims are later refuted by evidence. Einstein, directly responsible in large part for both Quantum Mechanics and Big Bang, rejected them both, accepting Big Bang only when the direct physical evidence became impossible to resist, and never really accepting Quantum Mechanics in its fullest form, despite having won his Nobel in QM. Even today, many reputable and respected scientists continue to resist both Big Bang and QM, and this in spite of the overwhelming evidence in support of both and complete lack of any contradictory evidence for either.

It is almost equivalent to the refusal by many religious people to accept evolution. Sir Fred Hoyle, Director of the Institute of Astronomy at Cambridge, rejected Big Bang by saying, "The passionate frenzy with which the Big Bang cosmology is clutched to the corporate scientific bosom evidently arises from a deep-rooted attachment to the first page of Genesis, religious fundamentalism at its strongest." It sounded entirely too much like religion for Hoyle to accept it, and he never did. Interestingly enough, his hypothesis, later shown to be true, that carbon production in stars was so unlikely as to need a "superintellect to monkey with physics, as well as with chemistry and biology"[3], sent him into scientific atheist crisis and caused him to believe in at least a god, if not the God, and in panspermia, illustrated by his statement that "The probability of

---

[2] www.alaska.net/~clund/e_djublonskopf/Flatearthsociety.htm

[3] Hoyle, F. 1982. The Universe: Past and Present Reflections. *Annual Review of Astronomy and Astrophysics.* 20:16

life originating at random is so utterly minuscule as to make the random concept absurd."[4]

When confronted in 1927 with evidence from his own General Theory by Belgian physicist (and priest) Georges Lemaître that the universe had to be expanding and must have had a beginning from a very tiny point, Einstein himself refused to accept it, saying "*Vos calculs sont corrects, mais votre physique est abominable*," that is, "Your calculations are correct, but your physics is abominable."[5] Hubble discovered in 1929 that the universe was expanding, and suddenly Big Bang became a legitimate explanation for the origin of the universe, ultimately to become the only explanation for which there was any scientific evidence. Eventually, Einstein (after a long wait, until 1933) is supposed to have said to Lemaître in front of the physics community, "This is the most beautiful and satisfactory explanation of creation to which I have ever listened."[6]

In truth, as I read in the debate between science and religion over origins, evolution, creationism, and all the rest of it, I find that both sides are making the same mistake—assuming that science is finished and that all of existence (by the one side) and faith (by the other) needs to be evaluated and understood according to current, right-now understandings of it all. The popular and loudest supporters of evolution are making the same assumptions made by Newcomb, Michelson and Kelvin at the end of the 19th century—evolution is complete, with just more and more precise measurements to be made that will inevitably support classical Darwinian and neo-Darwinian evolutionary models. We will not now nor will we ever find any evidence that will change the fundamentals, or so the assumptions go.

Though it is taking place behind the scenes and out of the public's view, the evolutionary movement is being forced to deal with revolutionary thoughts coming from evolutionary thinkers like Stuart Kauffman, the late Stephen Jay Gould, Niles Eldridge, Lynn Margulis, Eva Jablonka and Marion Lamb, among many others. As we demonstrated in the first book, determinism, mechanism, and reductionism still reign supreme after 400 years and despite the science of the 20th and 21st Centuries that showed them to be either tragically incomplete or completely tragic in describing the way the universe is actually put together.

Witness this excerpt from a *NewScientist* magazine editorial:

---

[4] *Evolution From Space*, Fred Hoyle

[5] Deprit, A. (1984). "Monsignor Georges Lemaître". A. Barger (ed) *The Big Bang and Georges Lemaître*. 370, Reide

[6] http://en.wikipedia.org/wiki/Georges_Lemaître

There is nothing new to be discovered in physics." So said Lord Kelvin in 1900, shortly before the intellectual firestorm ignited by relativity and quantum mechanics proved him comprehensively wrong.

If anyone now thinks that biology is sorted, they are going to be proved wrong too. The more that genomics, bioinformatics and many other newer disciplines reveal about life, the more obvious it becomes that our present understanding is not up to the job. We now gaze on a biological world of mind-boggling complexity that exposes the shortcomings of familiar, tidy concepts such as species, gene and organism.

A particularly pertinent example is provided in this week's cover story—the uprooting of the tree of life that Darwin used as an organising principle and which has been a central tenet of biology ever. Most biologists now accept that the tree is not a fact of nature—it is something we impose on nature in an attempt to make the task of understanding it more tractable. Other important bits of biology—notably development, ageing and sex—are similarly turning out to be much more involved than we ever imagined. As evolutionary biologist Michael Rose at the University of California, Irvine, told us: "The complexity of biology is comparable to quantum mechanics.[7]

That, however, will be the next book. This book is about how people of faith have also let determinism, mechanism, and reductionism define their understanding of their faith and their God, an understanding that is likewise tragically incomplete or completely tragic in describing our God and our faith. We too act as though our understanding of God and faith is complete, finished, only needing better measurement to confirm what we already think we know. This in turn defines how we respond to the assault raised by science on our faith and that raised by the new atheism. But vastly more importantly, it defines how we understand our interaction with God and our following of the faith.

What the reader, a person of faith, might be feeling at this point is threatened by the sneaky feeling that we are going to create a new faith in these pages, that we will take the old familiar faith and modernize it, retrofit it to our turbulent and challenging times so that it ceases to have any resemblance to that good old time religion.

In fact, our intent is to take us back to what the faith ought to be and was before we allowed ourselves (or rather the theologians and thinkers before us) to drift far off center and to recreate our faith as something it was never intended to be.

---

[7] Editorial: *Uprooting Darwin's tree*, 21 January 2009, NewScientist Magazine

We are not going where you think we're going, regardless of what you think. We're going to find the quantum God and the fractal Jesus.

*Glossary of Terms as they appear in the Introduction

Evolution:

Darwinian evolution proposes that complex life forms arrived from simpler life forms via natural selection, that eventually species separated to become new species, that this all happened gradually over immense periods of time, that there is no direction to evolution other than survival, that the fittest to survive will survive and those which are not fit will be marginalized or cease to exist. Darwin did not know how creatures adapted to changing environments so as to be able to survive better.

Neo-Darwinian evolution arrived with the discovery of the gene and of genetic mutations. Random mutations in the genome thus became the single operative engine that drove and continues to drive evolutionary change. Random mutations on one gene in one organism provide for a change in behavior or morphology (the physical body) that coincidentally happens as it is needed to provide for better survivability in the face of this environmental challenge, and also happens to be able to be reproduced in subsequent generations. Thus a community of new and better creatures gradually arises, replacing the old, less adapted community.

There is no other engine to drive evolutionary change in traditional neo-Darwinian evolution, and there is no explanation for the arrival of life from within evolutionary theory.

There are other proposals in modern evolutionary theory that suggest that random mutation and natural selection play a less significant or even a minor role in providing for evolutionary changes. See the section entitle "Extra Bits" on page 183 for several possibilities in this regard.

Creationism:

Comes in several flavors – young earth, old earth, Intelligent Design, and Fine-tuning. There is some overlap.

Young earth creationism: Everything was created in six days by God about 6000 years ago. The six-day creation cosmology comes from the Bible. The proposal that it happened 6000 years ago comes from someone called Bishop Ussher in the 1600s, who calculated the dates by adding up all the ages of the people in the Old Testament chronologies and subtracting backwards. Martin Luther and Johannes Kepler helped him with his calculations. More info on Ussher at www.law.umkc.edu/faculty/projects/ftrials/scopes/ussher.html .

Old earth creationism: Generally accepts an old earth and universe (4+ billion years for earth, 14.7 billion years for the universe) with a six-day creation cosmology. More info can be found at www.nwcreation.net/ageold.html and www.answersincreation.org.

Intelligent Design: Generally old-earth oriented; the major thesis is that biological organisms and systems appear too complex to have appeared without an outside design. Too many interrelated parts and pieces would have had to have arrived simultaneously in order to have provided for better survivability, and it doesn't seem possible for random mutation to provide for multiple mutations simultaneously that work so neatly together. The mousetrap from Lehigh's Michael Behe is the standard example. The best source of information on ID is found at the Discovery Institute's website, www.discovery.org .

Fine-tuning: First proposed by chemist Lawrence Henderson in 1913, extended by physicist Robert Dicke in 1961 and Fred Hoyle in 1984, modernized by John Gribbin and Martin Rees in 1989's *Cosmic Coincidences*, and supported in Christendom by Hugh Ross. Fine-tuning looks at the parameters of the existence of order, structure, and life itself to propose that it is physically and mathematically impossible for such an earth and universe to have arrived by accident. Within the secular physics community, fine-tuning is called the Anthropic Principle, proposed by physicist Brandon Carter in the '70s. It is controversial, not widely accepted, not universally rejected, and has been used to make critically important predictions in physics that have turned out to be accurate and true, specifically by Sir Fred Hoyle (carbon resonance) and Nobel Laureate Steven Weinberg (the cosmological constant). Both Hoyle and Weinberg were/are atheists.

Parameters of Fine-Tuning: There are dozens; you can find them on Hugh Ross' website, www.reasons.org.

Theory of Everything:

The Holy Grail of Science. Physicists, cosmologists, and everyone concerned with the origin of the universe would love to find a theory that unites the existence of everything in one neat theory, preferably in one simple, beautiful elegant equation. There is precedent for it: Einstein's $e=mc^2$ and $G_{\mu\nu} = 8\pi T_{\mu\nu}$ express with amazing elegance the most complex properties of nature in simple, beautiful forms, and it is the latter equation above that probably started the impetus in physics to look for the simple, elegant answer as the right one, and that when we finally are able to express the universe in a theory, it will be in a simple, elegant equation.

Big Bang:

Bluntly, the only theory of the origin of the universe for which there is any evidence to be found in science and nature. Though Einstein originally rejected the idea that the universe had a starting point, preferring with the rest of the science community to believe that the universe was eternal and immutable, it was his General Theory (the equation above, $G_{\mu\nu} = 8\pi T_{\mu\nu}$) that first suggested that the universe may have had a beginning point. Eventually he and nearly everyone else was forced to concede that it was true, and finally to become, if not comfortable with the idea, at least resigned to it. Briefly, the universe itself, space and time, arrived in a tiny tiny fraction of a second about 13.7 billion years ago, everything and the potential for everything arriving in a blinding flash of pure physics. It was rejected by science because it sounded too much like the first chapter of Genesis, and eventually rejected by many Protestants because it didn't sound enough like the first chapter of Genesis. Both science and Protestant Christianity continue to hope that evidence will be found to disprove Big Bang. No luck so far.

The Singularity – the General Theory of Relativity seems to say that the universe expanded super-rapidly out of what turns out to be an infinitely compressed point of pure energy potential called the Singularity. Every Black Hole is thought to contain a singularity, a place where the laws of physics not only break down, but in the case of Big Bang, the laws of physics actually originated. Space and time cease to exist in Black Holes, and Space and Time had their origin in Big Bang, so at the Big Bang Singularity, Space, Time, and the laws of physics, the fundamental forces of nature did not yet exist. The universe itself started from a dimensionless point that did not exist in space or time. Stephen Hawking and Roger Penrose are credited with much of the theoretical information about singularities. There are now several competing theories, one of them Hawkings' himself, that indicate an on-going struggle with concept of singularities.

Quantum Mechanics:

Also known as Quantum Theory and Quantum Physics, abbreviated by this book to QM. QM is the theory of the structure and behavior of atoms and subatomic particles. It arrived mostly in the first part of the 20th Century, and the more we discovered about the world of the very small, the more disturbing it became. The Quantum, micro-world is nothing like our large, macro-world, but everything is made of quantum particles.

Quantum particles can be in two (or many, or all) places at the same time, can travel immense distances instantaneously without having to cross any of the territory in between the arrival and departure points, don't have a real location in space or time, exist in a sort of quantum uncertainty where their realities have not yet been determined, and have realities that are only determined when a human attempts to observe them.

There are many upsetting elements to Quantum Theory, the most disturbing of which is the role of the outside observer. In a universe where to science humans seem to have no unique role at all to play, where we are no different than animals or anything else, for that matter, it seems to take a human observation of the quantum space in order for reality to exist. As much as nobody within quantum physics itself or the rest of humanity likes this, no one has ever been able to get rid of the need of the observer in creating reality at the quantum level, and since everything is made of quantum things, well, there you go.

If you'd like to do additional reading on QM (as though that would help), be sure to read about: The Two-Slit experiment (where one particle goes through two slits at the same time, and changes what it does depending upon whether or not you are looking at it); the Heisenberg Uncertainty Principle (which implies that a particle has neither a position nor a velocity until you look at it); Entangled Particles (which communicate instantly over vast distances), Quantum Tunneling (where particles skip from here to there without going anywhere in between), Schroedinger's Cat (where a cat is rendered neither alive nor dead by a particle that is not being observed), Quantum Computers (which are both on and off at the same time), and of course, the Copenhagen Effect (nothing ever happens without an observation). There is also Quantum Teleportation, Quantum Biology, Quantum Water, Zero-point energy, and the list goes on.

Here's what physicist Roger Penrose from Oxford says about Quantum Mechanics and, in passing, Relativity: "Quantum reality is strange in many ways. Individual quantum particles can, at one time, be in two different places - or three, or four, or spread out throughout some region, perhaps wiggling around like a wave. Indeed, the "reality" that quantum theory seems to be telling us to believe in is so far removed from what we are used to that many quantum theorists would tell us to abandon the very notion of reality when considering phenomena at the scale of particles, atoms or even molecules.

"This seems rather hard to take, especially when we are also told that quantum behaviour rules all phenomena, and that even large-scale objects, being built from quantum ingredients, are themselves subject to the same quantum rules. Where does quantum non-reality leave off and the physical reality that we actually seem to experience begin to take over? Present-day quantum theory has no satisfactory answer to this question. My own viewpoint concerning this - and there are many other viewpoints - is that present-day quantum theory is not quite right, and that as the objects under consideration get more massive then the principles of Einstein's general relativity begin to clash with those of quantum mechanics, and a notion of reality that is more in accordance with our experiences will begin to emerge. The reader should be warned, however: quantum mechanics as it stands has no accepted observational evidence against it, and all such modifications remain speculative. Moreover, even general relativity, involving as it does the idea of a curved space-time, itself diverges from the notions of reality we are used to.

"Whether we look at the universe at the quantum scale or across the vast distances over which the effects of general relativity become clear, then, the common-sense reality of chairs, tables and other material things would seem to dissolve away, to be replaced by a deeper reality inhabiting the world of mathematics."[8]

String Theory, Loop Quantum Gravity, Inflation, the Multiverse, the Cyclic Universe, the Ekpyrotic Universe, Hawkings' Flexiverse, the Self-organizing Universe:

Feel free to look these up on your own. Except for the multiverse and inflation, which we will define here and later, we're not going to talk about these much.

---

[8] NewScientist Magazine, *The Big Questions: What is Reality?* 18 November 2006 by Roger Penrose

Multiverse: An attempt by science to get around both Fine-Tuning and the need for an observer in QM, the Multiverse is a very large, perhaps infinitely large collection of other universes, within which our universe lies. There is no physical evidence for even one other universe, much less an infinitely large number of universes. But it remains an attractive option to many, as you will read. It is primarily derived as a concept from String Theory, for which there is also no evidence yet, Inflation, which has come under strong critical scrutiny of late, and Hugh Everett's Many Worlds interpretation of Quantum Mechanics, for which there is, again, no evidence.

Inflation: An unimaginably small bit of time (10^{-35} of a second) in the original second of Big Bang when the universe expanded unimaginably rapidly, and then slowed down again. Inflation is necessary to explain critically important aspects of our universe, but there are new and significant arguments against it.[9] From Alan Guth.

Special and General Theories of Relativity:

From Albert Einstein, the Special Theory in 1905 (along with four other earth-shattering papers), the General Theory in 1915.

The **Special Theory** redefined our Newtonian understanding of Space and Time, which change at high speeds (close to the speed of light), which are actually what the universe is made of (Space-Time), and which at the speed of light ceases to exist. That is, at the speed of light, all of time is experienced in a single instant, and all of space is compressed to two dimensions. "Space-time dilation" is the official name of what space-time does at high speeds.

The **General Theory** redefined our Newtonian understanding of Gravity with respect to Space-Time; that is, gravitational objects (galaxies, stars, planets, you and me and anything made of matter) cause gravity to exist and be experienced by warping and bending the fabric of space-time itself. Though we speak of gravity as a force, it's really geometry – space and time are bent like the surface of a trampoline when you stand on it.

---

[9] See "The Inflation Debate" http://www.scientificamerican.com/article.cfm?id=the-inflation-summer, Scientific American magazine, By Paul J. Steinhardt, April 6, 2011

Chapter 1

Aristotle, Newton, and Why Pretty Darn Good is Not Perfect

Aristotle saw the universe as being made from five elements—earth, air, fire, water and the ether, and as you can guess, he was mostly wrong. It's not to say that we don't have earth, air, fire and water, and ether is quite useful for getting your spleen removed, but you learned more than that by the third grade, I'm guessing. He was pretty convinced that he was right, and because he was a Smart Guy, everybody sort of went with it.

Isaac Newton did much the same thing. He figured out how the universe worked, and thinkers both contemporary and later used four terms to describe it—Infinity*, Determinism*, Mechanism*, and Reductionism*. Though we dealt with them in detail in the first book, we need to give you a bit of hint what they are all about again here. That's because, unlike Aristotle, Newton was mostly right, but like being *mostly dead (The Princess Bride* —one of the great physics films of all time)(OK, not so much), Newton was only mostly right, except where he was really, really wrong. It wasn't his fault, but it does matter quite a bit. His view of things does make for a dull and boring universe relative to the way it really is, so we'll need to know why it used to be dull and boring, but isn't any more.

Infinity seems easy enough, though it is an excellent example of the thorns that await. The universe was thought for centuries to be infinite in time and space, infinitely old, infinitely large. The Greeks seem to be the first people in antiquity to have described it thus, so it was thought to be in the 1600s by the community of "scientists" or, as they were more likely to be called, "natural philosophers," and so it was thought to be until 1929.

An infinite universe on the one hand spoke to the infinite nature of God, and on the other gave room for the wonders of the natural universe to have happened by random chance. When science, specifically Darwin and those who followed, began to postulate and then to find natural processes that could explain the origin of things, it was apparent that immense amounts of time would be required for everything to have happened by random accident. When science and religion went their more-or-less separate ways, scientists began to consider that not only did there have to be a natural explanation for everything in nature, but also that there couldn't have been any special circumstances to have aided in the process, that is, nothing that seemed miraculously well-balanced and timed. The quantum, cosmological, chemical, geological, biochemical, biological and finally anthropological events that occurred had to have proceeded naturally as a normal part of a functioning universe. There could be no divine intervention at any point in the process. All nature, all rules, all the time. Thus, immense amounts of time were needed. Thus, infinity, or something close to it. Ish.

What this says about God and our understanding of God we will talk about presently. But where it fits in with Newton is in particular with respect to the other three concepts, starting with Mechanism. Newton himself said, "Gravity explains the motions of the planets, but it cannot explain who set the planets in motion. God governs all things and knows all that is or can be done;"[10] he thought and conceived of the universe as a clock wound up by an all-powerful deity. The universe was a brilliant and beautiful machine that worked according to laws and principles that could be described mathematically. Newton's equations of optics and planetary motion were extraordinary and are still commonly used. The universe was indeed a place where the past could be described and the future foretold, because the math allowed us to do so.

We predict solar and lunar eclipses, the arrival of comets and asteroids, the motions of incredibly distant galaxies, stars and now planets all by way of Newton's equations, and we can tell where they were and what they were doing far into the past. In truth, the essence of a machine is *predictability*, and the essence of the universe and all of nature within it is *predictability*. Newton saw it as a perfect creation by a perfect creator.

Others, Newton's rival Leibniz among them, saw however that if the creation was perfect, then there was no need for God to intervene nor to play any role in the ongoing process of a universe being itself without that intervention being a tacit admission of imperfection, that something needed fixing. This absentee God came to be seen as absent and unnecessary altogether; the universe didn't need a creator or an overseer. It worked according to mathematical and physical rules and laws that created and supported reality in a predictable and comprehensible sort of way. Newton's God of rules was replaced by a universe with rules, and no God. It was an infinitely old machine that had no need of a machinist. It is predictable (mechanism), entirely predetermined (determinism), and completely capable of being understood in all of its parts (reductionism).

Of course, the tacit assumption was that God designed the universe to be perfect—the tension between the Church and Copernicus and Galileo, along with Kepler, revolved to a large extent around a perfect universe with perfectly circular orbits around a perfect earth. It's curious that this assumption, one that is not supported by scripture, became the starting point for getting rid of God altogether. It is still true—when evolution criticizes Intelligent Design, one of the criticisms is that when the designer God, who really should know how to make things, came up with some of his designs, they weren't really all that perfect. In fact, some of them were of pretty shoddy construction—the knee is a great example of a lousy example.

---

[10] Tiner, J.H. (1975). *Isaac Newton: Inventor, Scientist and Teacher*. Milford, Michigan, U.S.: Mott Media.

We are still rejecting God on the assumption that if he did the whole thing, he would have done it perfectly, and since it's not perfect, then God must not exist. That makes no sense. At best, one must reevaluate one's assumptions about God's intent for the universe, and perfection is clearly not a part of the picture. In truth, there were two critical levels of tiny imperfections in the early universe, two "broken symmetries" that were absolutely necessary for the universe ultimately to be able to have any order or structure at all—a 1/100,000 difference in the density of the cosmic background microwave radiation, and a 1 in a billion quantum mechanical imbalance between matter and anti-matter. The very earliest universe was necessarily imperfect in order for you and me to be here.

In fact, believers have to develop a new understanding of God's creation at this very point, perhaps our first point of a needed reorientation. Many of us will have made the assumption that the creation was perfect, when in fact (not to mess up your theology)(OK, maybe a little.) it was described as "good." God saw that it was good. Does that mean that everything was perfectly designed? I don't know, but there's no biblical mandate for perfection.

Clearly there were built-in limitations. The human eye, as brilliantly ornate and complex as it is, can see only on a very narrow spectrum of available energy waves, as shown below as "visible light." The largest part of the energy spectrum is invisible to us.

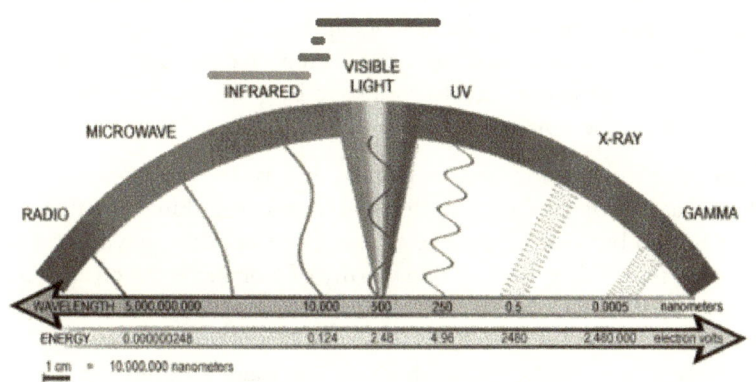

There are many things the human body cannot do: fly, jump immense distances, throw immense distances, run faster than a certain (pretty slow) speed, and so on. There are many things that the human mind cannot do, such as knowing all the tiny, chaotic variables needed to make accurate predictions, understand quantum realities, see into the future, teleport through walls, read minds, bend spoons. We cannot go as fast as the speed of light.

We could continue with a long list, but it's not necessary as long as we understand the issues. None of these things are imperfections—they are just limitations, and we are limited by nature to being what we are and can be, and no more.

Most importantly, we are not God, and that is the essence of our limitations and imperfections. We may want in our naïve arrogance to say that "nothing is impossible," but many things are impossible, perhaps most things. We can do amazing things; though we cannot float or fly in the air, we can build machines that will do those things for us. Though we cannot live for long underwater unaided, with aids we can stay for long periods of time underwater. Though we cannot see the infrared or the gamma ends of the spectrum, we can measure and record them. Though we cannot understand the quantum world, we can describe it very precisely.

But we are still limited, imperfect, not God, made to be not God, prevented from being God by God. And so we are not perfect, and so the creation is not perfect, lest we should worship it as God. The creation is not God, just for those who might have been tempted to worship fire, the sun, volcanoes, cats, or lovely actresses. It is not and can never have been perfect, though it is good. You are good, or have the potential to choose to be good, but you are not God, and you do not have the potential to be God.

I have read that the creation story in Genesis has as its prime goal to demonstrate that God is God overall, that he created everything, and that nothing else is God but God. It may be a message to all of those who would worship created things that the only one worthy of worship is the creator God. I am reminded of this when I hear today's scientists who deny God's existence encourage us to worship nature and the universe. Nobel prize winner Stephen Weinberg is one when he says, "Though aware that there is nothing in the universe that suggests any purpose for humanity, one way that we can find a purpose is to study the universe by the methods of science, without consoling ourselves with fairy tales about its future, or about our own."[11]

Carolyn Porco of the Space Science Institute in Boulder, Colorado is another, as was recorded in *NewScientist* magazine:

---

[11] "The Future of Science, and the Universe," *NYR*, November 15, 2001

If not God, then what? Science, she said, could do at least as well as religion. "If anyone has a replacement for God, then scientists do." Porco said. "At the heart of scientific inquiry is a spiritual quest, to come to know the natural world by understanding it... Being a scientist and staring immensity and eternity in the face every day is about as meaningful and awe-inspiring as it gets."

Astronomers in particular, she suggested, regularly confront the big questions of wonder. "The answers to these questions have produced the greatest story ever told and there isn't a religion that can offer anything better." Religious people, she claimed, use God to feel connected to something grander than they are, and find meaning and purpose through that connection. So why not show them their place in the universe and give them a sense of connectedness to the cosmos? The answers to why we are here, if they exist at all, will be found in astronomy and evolution, she said."[12]

Dr. Porco is head of the team that produces and analyses the Cassini photos of Saturn, as in the one at the end of this chapter.

Also in *NewScientist* is New Atheist Sam Harris, author of *The End of Faith*: "Let me offer the universe to people. We are in the universe and the universe is in us. I don't know any deeper spiritual feeling than those thoughts."[13]

And Neil deGrasse Tyson, astrophysicist, Hayden Planetarium, New York: "Let's teach our children about the story of the universe and its incredible richness and beauty. It is so much more glorious and awesome and even comforting than anything offered by any scripture or God-concept that I know of."[14]

But the universe is not God, though it may be glorious and awesome and maybe even comforting. It is not perfect, nor can we demand or expect perfection from it. And we are not God nor are we gods; we are not perfect, not capable of perfection on our own. My knees hurt and swell when I ski. I cannot see or read without glasses. Parts of my head have been exposed to the heavens and the earth. I have teeth in my mouth that I did not grow there. My feet are

---

[12] **Beyond belief: In place of God,** 20 November 2006, Exclusive from New Scientist Print Edition. Michael Brooks, Helen Phillips
[13] Ibid.
[14] Ibid.

flat and ruin good shoes. I have bad breath in the morning and gas at embarrassing moments. I cannot see microwaves or gamma rays, and I cannot hear what dogs can hear, nor do I have echolocation like bats and whales. No human ever could.

But the finite I can commune with, as we shall see, the more-than-infinite God, and that is his design and intent.

*Glossary of Terms as they appear in Chapter One

Infinity, Determinism, Mechanism, and Reductionism:

Infinity: The universe is infinitely old and infinitely large, no limits, no boundaries, no start and no finish. General Relativity spoiled this – the universe had a starting point in space and time, which we now call Big Bang.

Determinism: Everything that happens in the universe is caused by something else, which in turn was caused by something else. Everything is cause and effect, and in an infinite universe, there are an infinite series of causes and effects, with no original cause, no Prime Mover. Determinism removes any chance of free will from the universe. Quantum Mechanics spoils this, since at the quantum level, things happen without a cause, probabilistically rather than deterministically. And we are all made of quantum particles, so although many things are pre-determined, everything is not. Determinism also needs an infinitely old universe so that there is no need to have a First Cause.

Mechanism: The universe operates like a big machine according to rules, laws, mathematical equations, physics, chemistry, biology, and so on. Everything can be described by using the rules, and if enough information and data can be gathered, the outcome of any physical condition can be known, described, and fully predicted. Everything is predictable, including all of humanity and every individual within it. Each of us is entirely predictable. Mechanism is spoiled by QM, where things cannot be predicted, and by Chaos Theory (the Butterfly Effect), which shows that we can never know enough about any system to be able to predict what will happen because there are too many tiny variables that cannot all be known. The universe is fundamentally unpredictable.

Reductionism: Everything in the universe, in all of nature, can be understood by taking it apart, and the smaller the parts, the better the understanding. Ultimately, everything can be reduced to particles and their interactions; that is, everything any one of us might think or do at any moment of our lives can be reduced to particles and their interactions. Reductionism is spoiled by QM, since at the smallest levels, not only do we not understand things better, we don't understand things at all, and by Complexity Theory, which states that systems have emergent properties that cannot be predicted by breaking the systems down into their component parts.

Chapter 2

The More-Than-Infinite God

I'm going to venture out on the ledge here and speculate that everything you think about infinity is wrong. That will be true regardless of your faith position; atheist or deist, fundamental or progressive, Young or Old Earth, lover or hater of evolution, creationism and/or Intelligent Design, Christian, Muslim or Jew, Buddhist, Hindu, Jain, Confucian, Druid, Wiccan, Pagan, Heathen, Hedonist, or whatever. I'm happy and willing to be wrong. But the reason we don't understand infinity is because we don't understand time.

I'm betting that you are pretty much thinking that infinity has something to do with time in the sense that infinity is lots and lots of time, all the time that ever will be, the opposite of no time, as in, "I have no time for this."

Science was first to be wrong about time, and I should tell you that we still have no functioning, useful definition of what time actually is, outside of how it works in physics and cosmology, so it may not be the fault of science. Curiously, Augustine was closest to understanding time as it really is, though "is" is not exactly the right word to use about time. From the Cliffsnotes on St. Augustine's Confessions; the italics are mine:

> Augustine considers the meaning of the first words of Genesis: "In the beginning, God created heaven and earth." Augustine asks how he can know that this is true. It is obvious that all things were created, because they are subject to change. God created them through the Word, Jesus Christ. The Word is co-eternal with God and not created. People ask what God was doing in the time before he created the world. *Augustine replies that there was no time, because God created time itself.* Augustine considers the nature of time. One can speak of past, present, and future time, but *the past has ceased to be, the future is not yet, and only the present exists, but the present moment cannot have any duration.* But if this is true, how can one speak of history, or how can prophets foresee future events? The human memory retains images of past events. Perhaps some can predict the future by reading likely signs of what will happen. How do people measure time? The movement of the sun and planets is not time, as many assert. Augustine concludes that time is a "distension" of the mind; what human beings measure is the impression that things or events make on them. Augustine is torn and divided by time, but God alone is eternal and unchanging.[15]

---

[15] http://education.yahoo.com/homework_help/cliffnotes/st_augustines_confessions/68.html, Chapter Analyses - Book 11, Chapters 1–31

We'll come back to this.

As far as science was concerned, time, if nothing else, was that thing which is unchanging and eternal (sounds a bit like our traditional religious view, as well). Time was forever backward, forever forward, measured in numbers, but since time was infinite, the numbers by which we might choose to measure time are arbitrary and will change from age to age, epoch to epoch, culture to culture, society to society, but time itself was immutable and absolute. The universe was and is infinitely old, immeasurable except in the very short, very arbitrary range of numbers we use to assign age.

And then along came Albert Einstein and the Special and General Theories of Relativity. First he theorized that both space and time are bound together in what is the fundamental fabric of the universe itself, something called Space-Time. Now we have a problem: time is not something that passes. Time is part of what is, the structure of the universe, the framework that you and I and everything are built both on and out of. Time is not separate from us, something that we experience. Time, and Space, so Space-Time is what is, and everything that is, is Space-Time, made of Space-Time, part of Space-Time. (I am deeply befuddled.)

Further, as Augustine notes, time doesn't really exist in the way we think it does, as a sort of continuum of events, a life spent on the train tracks of time, every moment at one point on the tracks, with tracks stretching out behind us to our birth and in front of us to our deaths. No, the time that is behind us doesn't exist any longer—it's gone. And the time in front of us doesn't exist yet.

Worse, the time we occupy is…what? How long is each moment that we experience? Can it be measured? Does it have a length? If you think of it like a number line, full of points, you might notice that each point on a number line has no dimension, no size, no height, no width, no breadth, no volume. Each point is essentially pointless, if that makes sense, which of course it does not. And thus each point of time is pointless, without dimension. As a line somehow has length, even though it is made of things that have no length, an infinity of nothings adding up to something, so does time not exist, a lifetime of dimensionless bits of time that somehow add up to a lifetime.

Physics might try to tell us that the smallest unit of time is Planck time, 10^{-43} of a second, and that might be true. I don't think we actually know, though, if that is true in reality or just in a quantum sort of way.

Even more disturbing is to talk about Space in the same way. Space is just lots of points, and each point has no dimension. Somehow Space, like a line and a plane, attains real existence, even though it may be made up of things that don't have a real existence. Space-time then is made up of things that don't have dimension; we travel through space and time one dimensionless point at a time.

What's more, both space and time, Space-Time, change when you move. Well, they don't change absolutely—they only change relative to the place you started from. And they don't change very much, not in any really measurable way, until you start to move very very fast, at certain high percentages of light speed (which is just under 300,000 kilometers per second).

For example, if you have left the earth and are traveling in a space ship (more accurately called a space-time ship, though to my knowledge no science fiction writer has ever called one by that name) at 90% of the speed of light, you are aging at half the speed you would be aging on earth, and you are compressed in the direction you are traveling by 50% of your former size in one direction. 90% of the speed of light is a bit less than 270,000 kilometers per second—the fastest that humans have ever traveled is about 40,000 kilometers per hour, so we've not come close. 40,000 km per hour is a touch more than 11 km per second, so we are short by 269,989 km per second. If you stayed at that speed (back to 90% of the speed of light) for 10 years and returned to earth, everyone on earth will be 20 years older than when you left.

However, as you are able to increase your speed past 270,000 km/sec, the effect gets rapidly larger in a logarithmic sort of way, until, if you were able to actually hit the speed of light, time would stop passing altogether, in a sense. It's better to say that for you on the space-time ship, all of time will pass in a single instant, all of time compressed into no time at all. You would travel to the end of time.

Don't worry—we can't send you that fast. We are still limited to about 26 or 27 km/sec (94,000 km/hr), which is the speed of the Voyager 1 spacecraft that left earth in 1977 and is now about 16 million km from us (messages take over 29 hours to make the round-trip transit), so we are still 269,973 km/sec short of 90% of the speed of light, not of course the nearly 300,000 km/sec that light travels.

So science and normal humans, even abnormal humans like Isaac Newton, assumed that space and time were just what they looked like to normal humans, that is, pretty unchanging and unchangeable, Einstein demonstrated that what we thought was true was really just not true at all. And then it got worse.

He finished the Special Theory of Relativity in 1905, along with three other unbelievable papers (plus his dissertation), one of which (on the photoelectric effect) won him the Nobel Prize, though not until 1921 He didn't use the term "Relativity"—that came from Max Planck—but rather the Theory of Invariance, because the basic concept was that the laws of physics don't change anywhere for any reason. He was concerned that the term "Relativity" would free people to say that "everything is relative" in nature, including in culture, morality and ethics, and so on, which did ultimately happen.

Everything, as it turns out, is not relative at all. The absolutes of nature are absolutes everywhere at every moment, a proposition that has continued to be found true throughout the universe as a result of the evidence discovered in support of Big Bang.

It turns out in fact that Big Bang means that the universe is invariant, that the fundamental laws of physics apply throughout the universe in the places that we can see and in the places we can't. Those who would and have redefined morality to be relative by using physics to claim that everything is relative and there are no absolutes know nothing of physics—and perhaps nothing of morality, by extension. Of course, we don't use physics to rewrite moral codes, but those are the scientific roots, and they were wrong.

One is tempted to say that if God created a universe with absolute physical laws to define it, then the idea that there are also absolute, God-given moral codes has great credibility.

In 1907, Einstein started to try to integrate gravity into the Special Theory, something that proved to be quite a bit more difficult than just working with space and time. When he released it to the world in 1915, and when evidence to support it was found by Arthur Eddington in 1919, the stage was set for science to turn itself upside down and inside out. Without going through the details, the General Theory described in almost literally unbelievable detail and with astounding precision the way the universe is put together, and physicists began to work through the math.

First, Russian physicist Aleksandr Friedmann discovered in 1922 that the math of the General Theory meant that either the universe had to be either contracting or expanding, but it couldn't just be hanging around in an unchanging state, despite Einstein's strongly held view that the universe was static.

Then in 1927, as we have read, Lemaître did the math and proposed an expanding universe that began with a "primeval atom" about the size of the distance of the circumference of the earth's orbit around the sun, called an "astronomical unit," now seen as the precursor to the Big Bang theory, although the primeval atom turned out to be unimaginably smaller than Lemaître envisioned.

Einstein resisted, even introducing an awkward and ugly term, λ, *lambda*, that he called the Cosmological Constant, into the General Theory to try to force the universe to be static, until Edwin Hubble discovered the existence of galaxies and that the universe was expanding—an expanding universe has to be expanding away from something, a starting point, and now observational evidence dovetailed with the predictions of the General Theory. Einstein had to remove *lambda* from his equations, calling it the biggest blunder of his career.[16]

The universe had a starting point, and the General Theory would define it for us in ways that science has still not come to terms with and that many in the religious community refuse to accept. How can you not love a theory that (1) is fully supported by observational evidence, especially since Hubble's observations count as the most brilliant astronomical observations of all time, (2) is fully supported by mathematical and physical theory, particularly since it is the most brilliant theory ever discovered, and was roundly detested by both (a) scientists and (b) religion? In fact, many scientist, atheists, and religious people, especially conservative American Protestants, still dislike, distrust, disbelieve, or detest Big Bang. What a great theory!

Why didn't Einstein and the scientific community like it? As they investigated what the implications were, they discovered a host of really disturbing things. It wasn't that all the matter in the universe suddenly came into being in a pre-existent space and time. It was that space and time themselves came into existence with Big Bang. There was no pre-existent anything, not space, not time, not anything. It all came out of something they came to call the Singularity, which was an infinitely compressed point of pure energy potential, which is to say that not only was there no there for it to be there in, there was nothing to be there in the first place. No energy, just energy potential. No place in space —no space. No waiting for it to happen, since waiting happens in time, and there was no time.

And not only did we get space and time, space-time, a universe, a cosmos, we got it in a tiny tiny fraction of a fraction of a second—we got a universe-sized universe in far less than one second, everything springing from nothing for no apparent reason.

And there was no science to make it happen, because science and nature didn't exist yet. We had a brilliant theory matched by brilliant observations and (now) decades of evidence showing that everything came from nothing.

---

[16] "Astronomer Mario Livio has recently found that the "blunder" story is probably a myth." from **Your Biggest, Darkest Cosmic Questions Answered (Part 2)**, By Corey S. Powell | May 13, 2013, Discover Magazine blog.

There are essentially five things that run the universe: gravity*, the strong force*, the weak force*, the electromagnetic force*, and quantum mechanical interactions. The first four arrived with the universe, and we really don't know where quantum mechanics came from, though it really doesn't matter, since it will be both fundamental to the arrival of the universe and everything in it, and fundamentally incomprehensible. But gravity, the strong and weak forces, and electromagnetism did not pre-exist the universe nor co-exist with Singularity. They are created things, and they make everything happen.

Everything is a created thing. Nothing was not created—not science, not nature, not the universe, not the fundamental forces that run the universe, not the particles that mediate the fundamental forces. Nothing. In fact, there was not even nothing, not in the way we understand nothing, because for us, nothing is still something. Both something and nothing were created.

But even the fundamental forces don't make anything happen without matter, which is particles, and neither particles nor the universe itself exist without quantum mechanics, which worked in ways that, no matter how you look at it, are deeply disturbing.

Before we go there in the next chapter, let's consider the More-than-Infinite God. According to both Augustine and to Big Bang, *there was no time, because God created time itself,* as we read earlier. God is not infinite, not in the sense that he is all of time. Rather, he is outside of time altogether, and outside of space, in a place where we don't know how to go intellectually or theologically.

He is not bound by time nor by space, except when he chose to bind himself in the Christ-child. He became one of us in ways we can't even begin to understand—not just a human with human wants, needs, and temptations, but a creature captured in time and space, voluntarily imprisoned in four dimensions. When we describe God as infinite and eternal, we have limited him by our own lack of imagination and ignorance. He is not infinitely old, nor does eternity describe a place in time, or a time in space. It is something other, somewhere else, outside of us, apart from us. He created Space-Time as the vessel that contains us and the history he intends for us to inhabit.

He is, of course, entirely inaccessible to us except as he chooses to reveal himself. We are restricted in every way – intellectually, spiritually, scientifically – to four dimensions, with no way to conceptualize anything outside of those dimensions. We might imagine that there are more than four, as many have done, up to and including the ten or eleven (and at one point 26) dimensions of string theory into which gravity might be leaking, but we have at this point no evidence for them, and even if we did, our brains can paint no picture for us of dimensions outside our own.

The evidence in science that God, if he exists, exists outside of our universe is sure to be troubling to those who want to find, seek, or create God or gods within the universe. Not only can we not find him, we can't understand him or reduce him to something that can be understood, though the history of man is all about trying to reduce the incomprensible God to the comprehensible. The Grand Poo Bah of Atheism, Richard Dawkins, may have it right when he says to Francis Collins, "My mind is open to the most wonderful range of future possibilities, which I cannot even dream about, nor can you, nor can anybody else. When we were talking about the origins of the universe and the physical constants, I provided what I thought were cogent arguments against a supernatural intelligent designer. But it does seem to me to be a worthy idea. Refutable--but nevertheless grand and big enough to be worthy of respect. If there is a God, it's going to be a whole lot bigger and a whole lot more incomprehensible than anything that any theologian of any religion has ever proposed."[17]

Unless God had chosen to enter our universe and to reveal the parts of his nature and character through Christ as he did, then we would still be worshipping the sun or cats. Still, many refuse to see God in Christ. It is too easy to have claimed to talk to God. It is only when God enters our universe and shows himself to us in a way that we can both understand and be baffled by that the truth can be known. In space-time, as one of us, he is bound by time and space. Outside of space-time, he sees all of time in a single moment, all of history compressed into a moment of time without dimension, not just your own birth and death together with your entire life, but that of everyone and everything, from short-lived flies to ancient stars and galaxies. To God, all of time is instant, and all of space a point.

He is so much greater than we have allowed him to be.

---

[17] Time Magazine, **God vs. Science,** By Dan Cray/Los Angeles Sunday, Nov. 05, 2006. Read more: http://www.time.com/time/magazine/article/0,9171,1555132,00.html#ixzz0sGRcBEOf

*Glossary of Terms as they appear in Chapter Two

Strong Force, Weak Force, Electromagnetic Force, Gravity:

The theory of hot Big Bang Cosmology proposes that all four of the fundamental forces of nature (strong, weak, electromagnetic, and gravity) were bound together in the Theory of Everything (TOE), one force, and that as Big Bang progressed, each force crystallized out of the process. First, gravity separated itself from the TOE, leaving the Grand Unified Theory (GUT), which is the other three forces still combined. Second, the Strong Force popped out of GUT, leaving behind the Electroweak. Finally, electromagnetism and the weak force resolved into their separate selves. All of this happened in the first tiny parts of the original second. We have evidence that this is true for the Strong, Weak, and Electromagnetic Forces. We do not yet have evidence that Gravity was bound together with the GUT, the other three, because we don't yet have the technology to generate the energy levels needed to provide the evidence.

Each force has its own particles that "mediate" each, or cause each force to operate. The Strong Force is mediated by gluons. The Weak Force is mediated by W and Z bosons, whatever those are. Electromagnetism is mediated by photons and virtual photons (virtual particles are particles that are almost there, but not quite). Gravity is thought to be mediated by "gravitons", but little evidence has been found to document their existence yet. If gravitons don't exist, then physics is in a world of trouble.

The **Strong Force** is responsible for holding atomic nuclei together. Although it is very strong, it works over just the region that includes the nucleus in an atom. It provides small-scale structure that allows for matter to exist.

The **Weak Force**, or Weak Nuclear Interaction, is responsible for some forms of radioactive decay. The Weak Force has a major role to play in thermonuclear reactions, that is, the burning of stars, and thus a role to play in the arrival of the elements in the burning and death of stars.

The **Electromagnetic Force** holds protons and neutrons together with the nucleus to form atoms, and holds atoms together to form molecules. It also keeps solids from passing through each other via repulsion. Thus, it provides the everyday structure that we see around us and are a part of.

Gravity is the weakest of all the forces, 10^{33} times weaker than the next strongest force, but its reach is effectively infinite. Gravity is an interaction between things made of matter, which have mass, and space-time, and provides all of the large-scale structure in the universe. Everything made of matter bends space-time and therefore has gravity of its own, down to the smallest of atoms. We think of gravity as an attractive force field, in that things are attracted to one another via gravity. But gravity is in fact a geometrical warping of space-time by objects with mass.

Chapter 3

Nothing is Really Something, and Vice Versa

Having made a cosmos, God made one that was empty, and it's still pretty much empty. There's nothing really here.

Wait, I hear you saying, *I'm* here, and so are a lot of other people I know. Plus, I'm completely surrounded by things that are here, you know, like dirt, cars, houses, the odd bird and squirrel, and a whole planet full of stuff, not to mention the planet itself, the moon, the sun, the solar system, the galaxy, lots of galaxies. I mean, you told us there were maybe 200 billion galaxies out there somewhere, so don't tell me there's nothing here!

Sorry to disappoint you, but there's a lot more nothing than there is something in the universe, even if, as we acknowledged earlier, nothing is really something. We could almost say that there's so much nothing that it's really something, and so little something that it's really nothing. So the nothing is something and the something is nothing.

Perhaps I should clarify.

Let's start big. The observable universe is about 93 billion light years* across—there may be lots more universe out there somewhere, but we'll never see it and we'll never really know, and for our purposes here, it doesn't really matter. The universe is very large, and scattered across the universe are little lumps of matter gathered into things like superclusters of galaxies, clusters of galaxies, galaxies themselves, which are clusters of stars and star systems, and each star system, which is a little cluster of things like planets, moons, asteroids, comets, dust, and other things.

But there's a lot of empty space between superclusters, between clusters, between galaxies, between stars, and between planets and moons. If you happened to be hanging out somewhere outside of any galaxy between galaxies, the sky would be completely black – there would be no galaxy close enough to you to be able to be seen even as a point of light by your unaided eyes. No galaxies, no stars, no planets, nothing whatsoever to see. To you, space would be entirely empty.

Our galaxy, the Milky Way, has about 200-400 billion stars in it. It's 100,000 light years in diameter and 1,000 light years thick. If you want to do some math, just to figure out on average what the likelihood of finding a star in the Milky Way might be, here are the numbers: 100,000 light years is 600,000,000,000, 000,000(-ish) miles in diameter, and 1,000 light years is roughly 6,000,000, 000,000,000 miles thick. My computer calculator can't do that many zeroes, so I'm just going to say that the nearest star to us is over 4 light years away—24 trillion miles of empty space. I don't want to guarantee this figure, but when I did the math, it came out that the star density inside the Milky Way is about 1 star for every 3 thousand trillion trillion trillion cubic miles of space.

Our solar system has eight planets in it, and it is 2.8 billion miles to Neptune, now the outermost planet, from the sun. So there are eight planets spread over 5.6 billion miles, each planet occupying essentially a single point in its orbit. In the artist's impression below from NASA, you can see the sun in the far distance from a newly discovered planetoid called Makemake out beyond Neptune and Pluto, with a moon that may or may not actually exist. The sun at this distance is little more than a bright star, even though Makemake is still bound gravitationally to it.

There's pretty much nothing in the solar system, and there's pretty much nothing in the galaxy but empty space, along with a very occasional, really tiny clump of matter, and there's pretty much nothing between galaxies, since, well, you can guess that there is a lot of empty space between galaxies, and even more between galactic clusters and superclusters.

I believe that the average density of matter in the universe is four hydrogen atom (the smallest atom) for every cubic meter of space. Nobody has ever seen an atom, so that gives you an idea about how small they are, and let's say that 3 cubic meters is larger than a 9x9x9 foot room, a small bedroom with a higher ceiling. About 100 atoms in a room. How big is an atom? You have about 72 trillion cells in your body, each with 100 trillion atoms. Ish.

There's nothing here, on average.

Okay, now you might say, But everything that *is* here is *solid*, so that even if you average it all out with all that empty space, that doesn't seem fair, just because the matter that is here is all lumped up and concentrated.

Well. Not so much.

Back to the Bang. What the Big Bang left us with was a large (and getting larger faster) universe with rules, and after, or as the rules kicked in, depending on which rule you are talking about, there was that other little thing that we need in order for there to be order: matter in the form of particles. Some of the great unanswered questions in physics have to do with the appearance of matter

—why did we get matter, why did it hang around, and where did the anti-matter go?

We seem to have gotten matter because Quantum Mechanics gave it to us. One of the many strange things that QM does is take advantage of Einstein's most famous equation, $E=MC^2$, to turn energy into matter. In the very early moments of the first second of Big Bang, tiny particles were produced from energy, particles called quarks,[18] along with electrons and gluons (which stick things together inside the atom—that's why they call them "gluons.") Energy just becomes matter, pure energy into a contained form we call matter. Matter really is just energy contained. There's nothing solid to it.

Because the universe is a symmetric sort of place (Why? would be a good question), particles are produced with their anti-particles, thus, quarks and anti-quarks, electrons and positrons, gluons and anti-gluons. And when particles and anti-particles, which are just matter and anti-matter, meet each other, they each cease to exist.

So here's the question: knowing that we get matter and anti-matter in the early universe, and if they wiped each other out, then why is there any matter left? Wouldn't it have all been destroyed?

Quantum Mechanics seems to do something else for us. QM is all about probabilities, and it seems that there is a small probability that particles, every now and then, can arrive without their anti-particles. It's not very often, only one out of a billion times. But it was enough so that all the matter in the universe just popped into existence out of nothing for no reason, and it stayed around for no other than a tiny quantum mechanical chance that it would. Energy just became all of the matter we would ever have or need, and a one in a billion chance ensured that the matter would dominate over anti-matter in the universe. We're really not at all sure about how this happened yet.

This was finished at about 10 microseconds after the first second of creation was over, at which point quarks, which are prevented by the laws of physics from being alone, bound themselves (in groups of three) into protons and neutrons. With protons and neutrons, we had matter (atomic nuclei) and the potential for simple atoms (which would eventually include electrons). In terms of relative size, the visible universe is about 10^{18} bigger than the earth, the earth is about 10^{18} times bigger than an atom, an atom is about 10^7 times bigger than a quark, and a quark is about 10^{18} times bigger than a string, except of course nothing smaller than a nucleus really has a size, and strings may not exist at all.

---

[18] The term came from "three quarks for Muster Mark" in *Finnegan's Wake* by James Joyce, as whimsically chosen by Murray Gell-Mann, one of two man who theorized their existence, found them [sort of], and won the Nobel Prize for having done so.

Not only is matter just energy, but the amount of matter in matter hardly matters. Atoms are so small that nobody has ever seen one with any instrument of any kind. Quarks, which are glued together by a sea of (go ahead, guess) gluons to form atomic nuclei, are so small that we are not really sure they exist, and they certainly don't have any size. It is thought that they are 10^7 times smaller than the atoms they form, that is, the space they may occupy is that much smaller. They form the nuclei of atoms, but are only 1% of the mass of the proton, even though they are the only things in a proton. The rest of the proton's mass, 99%, is formed by virtual particles and anti-particles that spin into and out of existence on the order of nanoseconds.

The nucleus is so small relative to the size of the atom that if you enlarged a nucleus to about the size of a volleyball, the nearest electron would be eleven miles away, if an electron were actually anywhere at all, which it really isn't; there's a million billion times more empty space in an atom than there is matter. A nucleus is empty space. An atom (of which you have maybe 72 trillion cells worth) is empty space populated by things that, according to QM, are not really there, not in the sense we understand things to be there in. Electrons are not little balls of certainty but more like little clouds of possibilities. As QM genius Niels Bohr once said, "Everything we call real is made of things that cannot be regarded as real."

Space is empty. Matter is empty. Even the things that make matter up are not really even there. We have a universe that has the tiniest little percentage of matter in it, and matter has the tiniest little bit of energy in it. There's really nothing here except some energy.

And how much energy is in the universe? As it turns out, none. All the energy in the universe is from two types: positive energy and negative energy. Matter is positive energy. Gravity is negative energy. And they cancel each other out; there are 10^{50} tons of each in the universe. God took no energy at all and turned it into, well, I'm not really sure what he turned it into. Ultimately, he turned nothing at all into a universe with no net energy, and no net energy into the potential for you and me.

From a purely reductionist point of view, we're done. There is so little matter in the universe that it doesn't really matter. Just do the math. 100 hydrogen atoms per living room (with a high ceiling) and each hydrogen atom (and all the others) are made of things that don't really exist, plus a massive amount of more empty space. It's just emptiness, with every now and then a tiny little bit of virtually nothing but more empty space with some ill-defined energy bits whizzing about in clouds of possibilities.

But here is where reductionism fails its first test. For in all the vast emptiness of space and matter, the only thing that matters is matter, the tiny little particles and the interactions between them. Without matter, there is no order and structure in the universe, and in fact, there may be no universe at all. Matter may be nothing much, but as it turns out, not only is matter something, but matter is everything.

Let's review. Quarks, electrons, and gluons pop into existence (but not the type of existence you can understand or visualize), and as the universe cools (energetic photons [light] spreading out and losing energy), these particles start to interact according to the laws of physics. Each force (strong, weak, electromagnetic, and gravity) has its particles that come into being, gluons being the particles that mediate the strong force. Quarks are glued into atomic nuclei by the strong force.

The universe continues to cool for about 380,000 years, down to about 2,700° Celsius (roughly the surface temperature of the sun), the point at which nuclei can capture electrons via the electromagnetic force. Now we have simple atoms—mostly hydrogen, much less helium, and bits of some others—lithium, beryllium and an isotope, deuterium (which can only be created in this way and its existence in the universe is one more strong bit of evidence for Big Bang, along with the amounts of both hydrogen and helium, all of which match just what they should be).

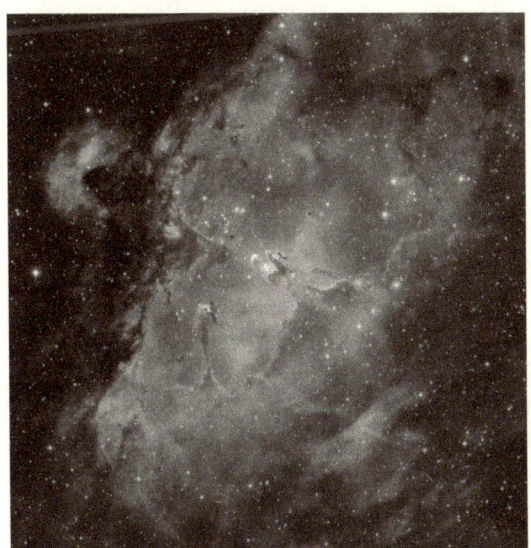

After 10 million years or so of the universe being dark, mostly empty, and void of activity of any type, gravity slowly kicks in and draws the atoms together into immense clouds of gas, like the one pictured, the Eagle Nebulae, one of the Hubble Space Telescope's most amazing shots.

The tiny little clouds at the center of the picture that look like fingers are 7 light-years long, 42 trillion miles. Gravity continues to draw these clouds together until pressure and heat rises, and eventually, as Barbara Streisand would affirm, a star is born. Star birth occurs because of gravity.

As stars burn under the intense heat and pressure of thermonuclear combustion, the rest of the elements, from carbon to iron, are formed in the fiery furnace. Eventually, the fuel burns out, or rather an imbalance between hydrogen and iron occurs, and the star, if it's big enough and again as a result of gravity, collapses and bounces out some of its material, eventually, over several generations of star birth and death, creating the rest of the naturally occurring heavy elements in the supernova, according to what have now become laws of physical chemistry, the process of producing all of the elements found in nature. The remaining core will become a white dwarf, a neutron or quark star, or even a black hole, depending on the size of the original star.

If there is a galaxy inside which this all happens, and this will happen pretty much just within galaxies, then other stars (gravity again) will capture the iron in orbits, iron that will round out into planets (gravity once more), and on the planets the chemistry we need for life will land: hydrogen, carbon, oxygen, nitrogen, phosphorous, silicon, all the things that life requires at the chemical level to exist, survive and thrive.

At this point we have a theological and scientific problem—the appearance of life. Many of you will expect me to talk about God creating life from dust (which under any understanding of nature is true; we are all made of stardust) as Genesis outlines it. Some of you will want me rather to go through the appearance of life via a natural process, perhaps alluding to the Miller/Urey experiments wherein amino acids were produced by running an electrical current through what is thought to have been a "primordial soup" of chemistry present on the early earth.

The Miller/Urey experiments, which I expect are still taught in schools, took place in 1953 on the basis of assumptions made about the chemistry of that primordial soup. In later years, scientists reformulated the chemistry of that soup based on new observations and discoveries. Miller himself repeated the experiment in 1983 with the new chemical mix, and got nothing.[19] That part of the story doesn't appear in textbooks, I'm thinking.

At this moment in time, we have in science absolutely no explanation for which there is any evidence for the appearance of life on earth. The situation is so desperate and the odds against life appearing by accident on earth so fearsome that many scientists are opting for something called "panspermia"— we were seeded from space, either by another civilization (less popular) or by the seeds of life that traveled by comet or asteroid to land here and gain hold to survive. Where those seeds of life originated is a problem that is not often discussed in science, though there is work being done in this regard.

As far as the biblical explanations are concerned, there are of course many different interpretations and opinions. Rather than risk sailing in those waters,

---

[19] "...the Miller-Urey (1953) results were later questioned. It turns out that the gases he used did not exist in large amounts on early earth. Scientists now believe the primeval atmosphere contained an inert mix of carbon dioxide and nitrogen - a change that made a world of difference. When Miller repeated the experiment in 1983 with the correct combo, the brown broth failed to materialize. Instead the mix created a colorless brew, containing few amino acids." www.sciam.com, March 2007

I'm going to give you the Quantum God in the next chapter. But first let's tie this one off.

You may have missed it as we rushed through our brief history of the universe, but if you were paying attention, you might have noticed that the only reason anything at all happened in the universe was because there was matter in it. Even though bits of matter are few and far between, and in purely reductionist terms don't exist in any meaningful way, the truth is quite the opposite: it is matter that matters and empty space that matters not at all. Bits of matter and the forces that interact between them have compelled the universe to get organized, to do something. Some of the great questions of physics and cosmology, of science in general, are these: Why don't we have just a big, empty universe? Why did the universe do anything? Why is there something rather than nothing?

It's one thing maybe to have little bits of matter floating around like rubble in the aftermath of the arrival of the universe in a great, roaring white flash, but why would those little bits of matter interact with each other and do things?

And the things they did are phenomenal—the most amazingly complex atomic structures, elements, gas, clouds, and then unbelievably, stars and galaxies, and more unbelievably, from the unimaginably powerful collapse and explosions of stars we get planets and star systems in neat little orbits, and the stuff of life, the physics we need for physical chemistry, the chemistry we need for biochemistry, the biochemistry we need for biology, and maybe above all the mystery elixir that turns chemistry into biology, that turns dust into life—water, so important that Lynn Margulis referred to life as "animated water."

And somehow we have all we need for life—the essence of life, and the things we need to support life, like water, energy, the ability to absorb and process energy and food, the ability to reproduce and change and adapt to environmental challenges, a process that produces increasing levels of complexity for no apparently rational reason, and finally, the most complicated thing in the known universe sitting between our ears.

Why would the universe do these things? Good question, but bad tie-off, is what I'm thinkin'.

*Glossary of Terms as they appear in Chapter Three

Light year – the distance that light travels in space in one earth year. Light travels at just under 300,000 km/sec (just over 186,000 miles/.sec), which is more than 7 times around the earth at the equator in one second, and 8.5 minutes to the sun. So that's:

1,080,000,000 km/hour (1 billion km/hr)

25,920,000,000 km/day (almost 26 billion km/day) and

9,460,800,000,000 km/year (almost 9.5 trillion km/year, or almost 5.9 trillion miles per year)

A light year is not a unit of time – it's a unit of distance.

Chapter 4

Quantum God

In order for there to be order in the universe, there has to be matter. That's not strictly true, because the universe had to do something else first, and second. First, it had to arrive, which is, as we will see, a quantum conundrum. Second, it had to arrive in a spectacular fashion, and by that I don't mean with a great big boom, or bang, as the case may be. That would be first. Second is that it had to arrive in an almost perfect state of thermodynamic equilibrium. What that means is that universe had to be the same temperature everywhere. Everywhere.

This is true because of something called entropy*, and entropy is something that always increases. That sounds like it would be a good thing if entropy were something you could deposit in a savings account, but unfortunately for most of us, entropy is pretty much the only thing we have in our savings accounts. Entropy doesn't mean "nothing" but rather "disorder." In the universe, order decreases and disorder increases, and that's a heat thing, not a socks-and-underwear-on-your-floor thing.

It's kinda like this: suppose you have a hot oven. Open the door. The heat escapes into the kitchen. Or suppose the bathroom is full of gas. Open the door. The gas escapes into the rest of the house, and gradually dissipates. Now wave your magic wand to try to get the heat back into the oven or the gas back into the bathroom. Won't work. Can't do it.

In order for the universe to have order in it now, it had to have more order in it a minute ago, and an hour ago, and yesterday and last week and last year and a million years ago and a billion and several billion, until you get back to the beginning of time and space, when the universe had to be at its most ordered state, the highest state of order that it would ever be in, almost the highest state of order it is possible to be in. Which is to say that as we go back in time toward Big Bang, the heat in the universe has to put itself back in the oven, so to speak. As it turns out, the further back in time we go, the more perfectly distributed the heat becomes, until we get to the very nanoseconds after Big Bang, when we discover that the heat distribution in the entire universe was almost perfect, perfect to five decimal points. That is, every place in the entire universe was exactly the same temperature as every other place in the universe, perfect to within $1/100,000^{th}$ of a degree.

This is remarkable, and as yet not fully explained by science apart from one theory called Inflation, which says that there was a tiny part of the original second (10^{-35th} of a second, a far smaller part of a second [by a power of two] than a second is a part of the age of the universe) when the whole thing expanded exponentially, thus spreading the heat evenly. It's a great theory, but it is still unproven and recently has come under some doubt. What we really have is a universe that arrived (still unexplained) that was almost perfect in heat distribution (ditto) to within one part in a hundred thousand, and that instantly produced all the matter we would ever need just because of a one-in-a-billion quantum mechanical chance that suggested that it might, two tiny places of almost imperceptible imperfection that turned out to be the pivot points for everything that happened afterward.

Because without matter, nothing would happen, but even with matter, if the heat distribution hadn't been nearly perfect, then the universe would have just started messy and gotten messier. Even then, if the heat distribution had been absolutely perfect, we would have had a great big universe with little protons, neutrons and electrons floating about randomly doing nothing.

And then it did what it did. And we still want to know why.

Let's talk about Determinism for a bit. M. Pierre-Simon Laplace is the scientist most directly given credit for giving us Determinism as a concept, in 1814. As we quoted him (in translation) in the first book,

> We may regard the present state of the universe as the effect of its past and the cause of its future. An intellect which at any given moment knew all of the forces that animate nature and the mutual positions of the beings that compose it, if this intellect were vast enough to submit the data to analysis, could condense into a single formula the movement of the greatest bodies of the universe and that of the lightest atom; for such an intellect nothing could be uncertain and the future just like the past would be present before its eyes.[20]

And so the assumption in science, and hence in philosophy, that the universe was entirely predetermined in all its parts, that the past could be completely known, the future totally predicted, all this limited only by computing power (of which there was none mechanically available in 1814, so this was an impressive assumption).

Note that the entirety of the assumption that the forces that interact between the greatest and the smallest bodies could be reduced to a single formula, that the largest objects in the universe (now known to be superclusters of galaxies), and the smallest of objects (now known to be the zoo of sub-sub-atomic particles inhabited by quarks and all its relatives) are intimately interrelated by the forces of nature, and that we can know all of these things in the past, present and future.

---

[20] http://encyclopedia.thefreedictionary.com/Laplace's+demon

Note as well that it was the tiniest of particles and the elementary forces of nature that started everything off in an amazing way. Tiny little particles acted on by incredibly weak—in one form or another—forces. The strong force is not weak, but it is only felt on a sub-atomic scale. Gravity is felt across the universe, infinite in its reach, but it's the weakest of the forces, 10^{33} times weaker than the next strongest force. On a universal scale, even electromagnetism has a limited reach, and the weak force again is just atomic in its reach. And yet these, acting on quarks and electrons, on protons and neutrons, on tiny little atoms of energy, moved inexorably down a path toward profound order in a constantly disordering universe.

So was Laplace right? Was it all inevitable, predictable, infinitely knowable?

In spite of the power and subtlety of the interactions between forces and particles and the elegant dance they performed and continue to perform, there is a mystery that Laplace could not have known or predicted that sits at the heart of nature. It is the quantum mystery, and it is the most bizarre thing known to man.

We each of us tend to make a great, unrealized assumption about the nature of reality, and that is that the reality we see and experience is the actual reality. Kant wrote of this in his inscrutable *Critique of Pure Reason*: you and I assume that what we see is what we get. We've already punctured this somewhat above: we assume that solid things are solid, that real things are really real, that I'm real, that you are real, that if I can see it, hold it, taste it, touch it, smell it, hear it, experience it, then it is a part of reality. We said that the universe and matter are essentially empty, but that it is the places where they are not empty that matter, and we made some allusions to things like quarks and things that don't exist in quite the way we would hope. But we have yet to begin to touch the quantum mystery.

By way of introduction, here's what the quantum guys themselves say about QM:

- "Quantum mechanics is magic." Science writer Daniel Greenberger.
- "Everything we call real is made of things that cannot be regarded as real." Niels Bohr.
- "Those who are not shocked when they first come across quantum theory cannot possibly have understood it." Niels Bohr.
- "If you are not completely confused by quantum mechanics, you do not understand it." John Wheeler.
- "It is safe to say that nobody understands quantum mechanics." Richard Feynman.

- "If [quantum theory] is correct, it signifies the end of physics as a science." Albert Einstein.
- "I do not like [quantum mechanics], and I am sorry I ever had anything to do with it." Erwin Schroedinger.
- "Quantum mechanics makes absolutely no sense." Roger Penrose.[21]

In 1900 Max Planck made one of the most important discoveries in the history of scientific inquiry: he found that energy had to travel in what one might call little lumps rather than, or in addition to, waves. It had been assumed based on volumes of experimental evidence that energy traveled in waves, but there were times when the assumption of waves didn't work. Planck discovered that energy had to move in packets he called "quanta," and suddenly we had a problem: energy moved in both waves and pieces.

In 1905, Einstein furthered the field of Quantum Mechanics by finding that light also was composed of quanta, as well as moving in waves. For you and me, this was not that big a deal. We would have no problem with light particles traveling in waves. After all, water droplets travel in waves in the ocean, cars travel in waves on freeways, people travel in waves on streets. Conceptually, we were not troubled. That would be because we didn't really understand what was going on.

As the field progressed through the 1930s, it got more and more weird, more strange, more bizarre, more unbelievable, until those who were paying attention realized that our classic assumptions about the way the universe was put together were fundamentally false, and what was worse, we couldn't understand anything about how it was actually put together.

At the risk of confusing us all further, let me quote Einstein as he tries to put it all together: "When forced to summarize the general theory of relativity in one sentence: Time and space and gravitation have no separate existence from matter. ... *Physical objects are not in space, but these objects are spatially extended.* In this way the concept 'empty space' loses its meaning. ... The particle can only appear as a limited region in space in which the field strength or the energy density are particularly high,"[22]

So for starters, particles don't exist as little bits of matter separate from space-time. Particles, along with everything that is made of particles (including you and me), are just an extension of space-time, a bulge of extra energy like a lump of mashed potatoes or Cream of Wheat, just space-time extra-thick, collected in little space-time lumps.

---

[21] all quotes from http://phys.wordpress.com/2006/06/09/quantum-mechanical-quotes/, physics musings
[22] www.spaceandmotion.com/quantum-theory-max-planck-quotes.htm

Wait. It gets worse. Much worse.

Without going through the excruciating details (we tried that in the other book, and we're not completely sure it worked very well in that one), here's the thing: All of these little lumps of space-time, these particles, don't behave in any way like the big lumps of space-time that we see and experience around us all the time, lumps like you and me. You and I, to be clear, stay in one place until we are ready to go to another place. We are never in two places at the same time. We never go from one place to another without covering all of the territory in between the two places. And when we go from one place to another, we take one path, not two or three, and we certainly don't take every path in the universe in trying to find the best path to take. When talking to people we know, we let ourselves, without ever really thinking about it much, be restricted by the speed of light or sound or phone lines, and certainly by time. We never ever go backward in time. Of all the things we don't do, we don't go faster than light, and we don't go backward in time.

Quantum particles, on the other hand, have an entirely different point of view. Photons, electrons, atoms, sometimes even molecules do all of those things on a regular basis. Particles are not quite particles, not quite waves, sort of both depending on how you are looking at them. At times, particles are in two places at the same time, sometimes in all places at the same time, sometimes traveling all possible paths in a search for the best path of all. And when we say all possible paths, we mean every possible path in the universe. Instantaneously.

Particles also communicate (weird enough just by itself) instantaneously across potentially vast distances at speeds hugely exceeding the speed of light. In fact, "instantaneously" means exactly that: it takes no time at all for the message particles to make the journey. Particles communicate using other particles, and the other particles are just that, particles, made of matter, and they travel faster than light.

Albert didn't like this very much, because it seems to violate special relativity. No, that's not right. It really does violate special relativity. Nothing made of matter can go even as fast as light, much less far faster. But at one point in the experiments involving what are called "entangled" particles, they seemed to be communicating, if memory serves, at 300 million times the speed of light, which is pretty darn fast, but not as fast as what the experiments now seem to be showing: they communicate in no time at all.

Particles also "quantum tunnel" from one place to another. That means that they go from here to there without going anywhere between here and there, like going from Brooklyn to New York without crossing the Brooklyn Bridge, one end to the other without using the actual bridge-y parts. They do this instantaneously, too. It's eerie.

Eeriest, weirdest, strangest, and most controversial (though universally accepted with great reluctance as true) is what is called the Copenhagen Interpretation of Quantum Physics. It may and certainly seems to involve backwards time travel, which is, oddly enough, not the most controversial bit. The most controversial bit is that the particles seem to change what they are doing, and how they are doing it, based on whether or not a human is looking at them, that is, trying to measure them in some way, most specifically trying to catch them doing things that they only really do when humans are not looking. If you want to catch them acting like particles, they'll do that, but when you stop, they'll start acting like waves.

OK, fine, but when you then try again to catch them acting like waves, they'll resume acting like particles, and they'll do it backwards in time if needed, back as far as billions and billions of years across vast reaches of space. And the Copenhagen bottom line is that reality is created when an observation is made, and not before. Reality does not exist without observations, and therefore not without observers. We determine the existence of reality itself.

That's not trivial, and it needs explaining. Our assumptions from Newton and from just looking around at nature are that things just exist. There may be relationships between things (we eat them, they eat us, whatever), but if humans weren't on the planet or in the universe, clearly the planet and the universe would still be here. Right?

Ah, not so much, as it turns out. Our assumptions are wrong, as it turns out. Common sense observations of the universe are, as it turns out, common nonsense.

The uncommon sense of the thing, purely and simply, if neither pure nor simple, is that since the universe is made of quantum particles, and every quantum particle requires something sentient, self-aware and intelligent to interact with it in order for it to become real, then the universe itself needs sentient, self-aware, intelligent beings in it in order for the universe to become real. You might feel like we've suddenly fallen into *The Little Prince* or *The Velveteen Rabbit*, or maybe rather *The Electric Kool-aid Acid Test*, but in fact, we've really just jumped down the Rabbit Hole, fallen into the Looking Glass, taken the Red Pill. Though *The Matrix* is not an accurate representation of what the universe is all about, it's a lot closer than what you might think. What you see is not what you get. Reality is in fact reality, but it does not come from reality. It comes from possibilities, and all the possibilities co-exist until the observation is made. Then they all, but one, go away.

The reality is, there is no reality without observation, and there is no observation without observers. Those could be Martians, Venetians, ETs, Klingons, Narnians, or the Wicked Witch of the West, but absent evidence of any of those, we are left with we. Us. Whatever. We are the observers that the universe needs to exist.

It might be helpful to tell you that nobody likes this, but that Quantum Mechanics is the finest field of science known to man (along with Relativity), the most experimentally validated field of science that exists, has never been shown to be incorrect, fully describes everything in the known universe, and apart from being incompatible with Relativity (now there's an interesting problem) is unbelievably accurate and essentially unbelievable. You might go back to pages 49-50 to see what scientists think about it. We'll also talk more about it in the next chapter.

To sum up, we are each of us made of quantum particles, lots and lots of them. I am made up of about 72 trillion cells composed of 54,200,000,000,000,000,000,000,000 atoms, and I can't even do the math for how many quantum particles. Each quantum particle can be in two (or many or all) places at the same time, can go backward and forward again in time, can skip from here to there without covering anything in between, can communicate instantaneously across the universe, and seems to be aware that we are looking at it and changes its behavior accordingly. But we can't do anything of those things, even though we are made of particles that can. Right?

Maybe. Maybe not.

*Glossary of Terms as they appear in Chapter Four

Entropy – the amount of disorder in a system. Entropy always increases in the universe, which means that the universe is always going from more ordered to less ordered. It's kinda like a house with teenagers. If you start with a pristine, brilliantly clean and ordered house, and insert some teenagers, well, you know what tends to happen pretty quickly. That's a metaphor for entropy – the house goes from ordered, neat and clean, to disordered, messy and dirty.

In a brand new house, just built, never lived in, you can tell by looking at it that it's new. No marks on the wall, no stains on the carpets, no dings on the door. If it's a used house that you are moving into after the previous owners moved out, they may have cleaned it really well, but there will still be little bits of evidence that it's not new. After you move in and live awhile, still more evidence that it's lived in. And if you have small children and pets, then the evidence begins to mount.

So it is with the universe. Our new universe was almost perfect (though it clearly didn't have to be, and we don't know why it was that way), and the older it got, the less perfect it became. That is, the new universe was almost perfectly the same temperature and density everywhere, but our present universe has really hot places and really cold places, really dense places and really empty places. It's older and has a lot more entropy.

The question is, with everything getting more disordered all the time, how do we end up with ordered things like galaxies, planetary systems, and you and me? The answer is, the laws of physics take the universe into more entropy, but along the way, those same laws cause things to clump together in bunches of disorder. You represent more disorder in the universe, but in a wonderful way, the laws of nature have produced the most ordered, complicated thing in the universe in that process – the human brain.

Chapter 5

Quantum God in Two Chapters at the Same Time

As it happens, the lines are not so clearly drawn.

Quantum Mechanics is all about probabilities, and there are some uncomfortable truths lurking down in its depths. One is that even if something seems unbelievably unlikely, QM allows for extremely unlikely things to happen, and not only allows for them to happen, but they just do happen. The smaller the object, the more common it is for unlikely things to happen.

But another uncomfortable truth is that even as the probabilities increase as things get smaller, they decrease as things get larger, but they never really go to zero. That is, these unlikely things can happen to macro-objects, too. The chances that weird, quantum things will happen to large, everyday objects are so small that we can't really consider that they will happen in the lifespan of our universe, but one never really knows. After all, the universe itself popped out of a quantum fluctuation, or so it seems, in an unpredictable and as yet ultimately indefinable sort of way. If a universe can just appear out of nothing, then QM's possibilities for similar things to happen on a smaller basis are not quite so unreasonable.

And so it does have those predictions. It is possible, though unlikely, for a human to be able to go through two doors at the same time, that is, possible to be in two places at once, at least according to *NewScientist*:

> How would you like to be quantum? It would certainly have its advantages. Imagine, for a start, if you could be in two places at once. Jet off to the beach and stay in the office at the same time. Do the weekend shopping and mow the front lawn simultaneously. Sure, you say, dream on.
>
> Well then, here's the shocking bit: you really could be quantum. After all, you are made of atoms and molecules that obey the rules of quantum theory. They can be in different states, spinning this way and that, all at the same time. They can be here, there and everywhere in between. The big question is why atoms can experience the full weirdness of quantum mechanics, whereas you and I evidently cannot. "In short, how does the well-behaved, everyday classical world emerge from the schizophrenic quantum realm," asks Johannes Kofler, a specialist in quantum theory from Caslav Brukner's group at the University of Vienna, Austria.
>
> We may finally have the answer. For years physicists have tried to pin down the elusive boundary between the quantum and classical worlds.

Now Kofler, Brukner and others have shown that this boundary may not exist. That's right, the quantum world never breaks down. If that's true, we're left with a mind-numbing prospect: the world could be quantum, but we are blind to it. This result challenges our very notions of how classical reality arises.[23]

We have to emphasize that for any of us to become quantum in a quantum sense is extremely hard and unlikely to do, but it's not impossible. Our assumptions of reality are just that; assumptions that are not true in the sense that we thought they were.

Just to illustrate how strange it all is, there is the possibility of something called Boltzmann Brains in the universe, this from the *New York Times*:

> It could be the weirdest and most embarrassing prediction in the history of cosmology, if not science. If true, it would mean that you yourself reading this article are more likely to be some momentary fluctuation in a field of matter and energy out in space than a person with a real past born through billions of years of evolution in an orderly star-spangled cosmos. Your memories and the world you think you see around you are illusions.
>
> This bizarre picture is the outcome of a recent series of calculations that take some of the bedrock theories and discoveries of modern cosmology to the limit. Nobody in the field believes that this is the way things really work, however. And so in the last couple of years there has been a growing stream of debate and dueling papers, replete with references to such esoteric subjects as reincarnation, multiple universes and even the death of spacetime, as cosmologists try to square the predictions of their cherished theories with their convictions that we and the universe are real. The basic problem is that across the eons of time, the standard theories suggest, the universe can recur over and over again in an endless cycle of big bangs, but it's hard for nature to make a whole universe. It's much easier to make fragments of one, like planets, yourself maybe in a spacesuit or even — in the most absurd and troubling example—a naked brain floating in space. Nature tends to do what is easiest, from the standpoint of energy and probability. And so these fragments—in particular the brains—would appear far

---

[23] From issue 2595 of *NewScientist*, 17 March 2007, pp. 36-39

more frequently than real full-fledged universes, or than us. Or they might be us.[24]

So what really could happen is that things as complicated as brains or even entire humans could just pop into existence out of the quantum nothingness. Nobody really wants this to be true, and they are working hard to show that it isn't, but it still is. After all, it is easier to make a brain or a human than it is to conjure up a whole universe, and that has already happened, so conjuring up humans is a piece of quantum cake. A large, hard-to-swallow and even harder-to-digest cake, but it's only hard for *us* to swallow and digest.

The universe is not like you and me. It's weird. Actually, we might be the weird ones. We persist in thinking that we are normal, but frankly, the evidence points in the other direction. We are like babies staring up at the ceiling from our happy little cribs, fully convinced that the world is composed of the mobile dangling above us and that we are fully aware and in control of that world, when in fact we haven't got much of a clue. We are watching a very lively four-dimensional film that we assume reveals reality to us, but we only see the reality we see. It's not the real reality.

One more thing about that real reality. As we wrote in the previous chapter, reality does not exist without observers, without observations. Nobody likes this very much either, and everybody from Einstein on down argued with Niels Bohr about this, but Niels won all those arguments. Even today, those who don't like it, such as Murray Gell-Mann, find themselves reduced to trying to define what happens after an observation is made, unable to do away with the need for an observation itself.

The problem then arises with how to deal with the universe before humans arrived on the scene. Did the universe exist at all? Gell-Mann finds the question ridiculous:

> Gell-Mann also continues to work on at least one physics problem—an interpretation of quantum mechanics that is suitable for quantum cosmology. However, he is no fan of the standard or Copenhagen interpretations of quantum theory. "The idea that quantum mechanics depends on having a physicist outside the system making repeated measurements—or measurements on repeated copies—is clearly absurd when you are talking about the universe," he says. "Is it

---

[24] The New York Times, January 15, 2008

imaginable that in the 13 or 14 billion years before human life appeared there was no quantum mechanics? That is ludicrous."[25]

As brilliant a physicist as he is, there are those who disagree, like Andre Linde of Stanford:

> Thus we see that without introducing an observer, we have a dead universe, which does not evolve in time. ...We are together, the universe and us. The moment you say that the universe exists without any observers, I cannot make any sense out of that. I cannot imagine a consistent theory of everything that ignores consciousness. ... In the absence of observers, our universe is dead.[26]

John Wheeler says,

> We could not even imagine a universe that did not somewhere and for some stretch of time contain observers because the very building materials of the universe are these acts of observer-participancy. You wouldn't have the stuff out of which to build the universe otherwise. This participatory principle takes for its foundation the absolutely central point of the quantum: "No elementary phenomenon is a phenomenon until it is an observed (or registered) phenomenon."[27]

Now we have to try to understand this from our human perspective and try as well to figure out what it says about God, especially the Quantum God. Piece of cake.

Not.

The quantum defines everything in science and nature. All of natural reality is defined by quantum realities. The universe apparently started according to quantum rules and proceeded along its path, guided at its very base and structure by those rules. As we have two rules that define Christianity (love

---

[25] http://physicsworld.com/cws/article/print/17564 by Peter Rogers
[26] *Does the Universe Exist if We're Not Looking?* by Tim Folger, published online June 1, 2002 By *Discover* magazine
[27] Cosmic Search Vol. 1 No. 4, www.bigear.org/vol1no4/wheeler.htm

God, love others) and all of life is supposed to be defined by those two rules, so is all of life, the universe and everything defined by quantum rules which are, pretty disconcertingly, not as easy to understand as those two rules, not in any sense.

To have a universe at all, that is, before the universe was here, there was the Singularity out of which Big Bang arrived. With Big Bang arrived space and time, space-time, so before Big Bang there was no before. Time and space did not exist.

But we seem to need an observation for Big Bang to have happened, and that observation had to happen outside of space-time as we know it. I'm not sure how that works, since science tells us that observation happens in space-time, that is, with an exchange of particles over a bit of space and inside a fragment of time. In our experience, observation needs particles to mediate the forces, forces to be mediated, and objects made of particles (observers).

If an observation needed to have been made in order for Singularity to become Big Bang, then that observation had to have happened in a way that is outside our ability to describe it. And yet I have never heard of Big Bang being referred to in any other way than as a quantum event. It is science's assumption from physics and cosmology that Big Bang was quantum.

So we are forced to accept Big Bang as a quantum event, at least for the moment. And that means that we needed an observer and an observation that existed and happened outside of four dimensions of space and time, outside of the four fundamental forces of nature, outside all of our familiar physical laws and constraints. We can't even understand the physical definition of this observation—no particles, no forces, no particles mediating forces, nothing happening in time or space. All we can say is that it represented some form of interaction between the observer and Singularity, recognizing that Singularity was a dimensionless point of pure energy potential that is much more accurately described as being nothing rather than something.

If you are happy ascribing the parameters of this event to "God," then it seems to fit a general description of something that looks and sounds like something that ought to be called God. If you think, on the other hand, that this is just one more example of a "God of the gaps" explanation for something we can't yet explain, then you are going to have to be satisfied with the need for an observer, the characteristics of whom (or which) we can't yet (and most likely will never be able to) describe, but who (or which) had to exist (whatever that means) outside of four dimensions of space and time, accompanied by none of the physical laws and forces that we live under.

One might note that "existence" is also defined in terms of space and time, that is, "existence" is to be occupying space for a period of time, or to use better physics, occupying a bit of space-time and being impacted by the forces and laws of nature over space-time. Our observer doesn't match those parameters, so even to talk about "the existence of God" is to impose restrictions on God that don't apply until he wants and/or chooses them to do so.

Paul Davies writes,

> I belong to the group of scientists who do not subscribe to a conventional religion but nevertheless deny that the universe is a purposeless accident. Through my scientific work I have come to believe more and more strongly that the physical universe is put together with an ingenuity so astonishing that I cannot accept it merely as a brute fact. There must, it seems to me, be a deeper level of explanation. Whether one wishes to call that deeper level "God" is a matter of taste and definition.[28]

And of course when, in our context, we use the word "God," we impose our own understanding of God on that word, and thereby limit God to being something we can understand. It should be clear by now that as we cannot understand the quantum, so we cannot understand God, except insofar as the quantum and God allow us to have understanding, an understanding that will necessarily be limited but powerfully useful.

Lest you think that I am capturing God inside the quantum and making him subject to it, I am not and do not intend to do so. God is the God of all, and thus he is God of the quantum. That means he is not bound by the quantum, although we are. There is one special place where I think that holds true in a way that applies directly to us and our understanding of and relationship to God.

Paul Davies also said, as a part of his paragraph above, "I have come to the point of view that mind—i.e., conscious awareness of the world—is not a meaningless and incidental quirk of nature, but an absolutely fundamental facet of reality."[29] The interaction by the human, conscious mind with the universe is what gives the universe its potential and reality, as we saw above, though not all scientists agree by any stretch of the imagination. Mostly they don't agree because it sounds so outrageous rather than because the physics is bad. (It does sound outrageous, but in a quantum universe, that's no reason to reject anything at all.)

---

[28] *The Mind of God*, London: Simon & Schuster, 1992
[29] Ibid.

But we have a problem. Humans didn't come on the scene until very recently in the history of the universe. Really, as far as being conscious is concerned, modern humans maybe came as recently as 100,000 to 250,000 years ago, according to the Mitochondrial Eve theory (see page 136 for more details on this). And that's assuming that we don't actually need a quantum physicist to interact with the quantum in order for reality to exist, as Gell-Mann implied above.

Thus the universe existed for the vast majority of its total age without any observers. And Quantum Mechanics tells us that it couldn't have done so. So we have an issue. Was it here or not? *Discover* magazine asked the question (in footnote 24 earlier), "Does the Universe Exist if We're Not Looking?" in June 2002. *NewScientist* magazine asked almost the same question in its 23 June 2007 issue on the cover, "Does the universe exist when nobody is looking?" The answer seems to be apparently not, not if Quantum Mechanics is true, and if there is anything that is true in science, it is Quantum Mechanics.

There are some options:

One, Quantum Mechanics didn't exist with Singularity and we didn't need an observation. That doesn't seem to be the common consensus within the science community, and it doesn't help much, since it leaves us with no explanation from science for the origin of the universe. We could all live with that, but nobody really wants to.

Two, from John Wheeler, observers are necessary for the universe to exist. His original thought was that the universe existed in a quantum state of uncertainty until humans were produced and interacted with it, whereupon the wave function collapsed backward in time to Big Bang, and reality came into existence. In this, we recognize that within the quantum, the past is affected by the present, so this may be possible. I understand that later in his life, Wheeler backed away from this, but that's hearsay until I can track it down.

Three, there are multiple universes, and this is the one that happens to have observers in it. I'm not sure how this solves the problem, since universes without observers don't actually exist, but lots of scientists like this one, so we'll include it. There are other variations on this theme: pocket universes, M-theory with five-dimensional membranes, the multiverse, the 10^{500} possible universes of string theory, and so on, but as we remember, there is no evidence for any of these. One possibility is from Hugh Everett who postulated that every time an observation is made, the universe divides itself into two universes, both possible universes attaining a separate reality. This doesn't really solve the observer problem, but again, there are those in science who like it.

It creates a fascinating tension, though as revealed by this from *NewScientist*:

What would you rather believe in, God or the multiverse? It sounds like an instance of cosmic apples and oranges, but increasingly we are being told it's a choice we must make. Take the dialogue earlier this year between Richard Dawkins and physicist Steven Weinberg in Austin, Texas. Discussing the fact that the universe appears fine-tuned for our existence, Weinberg told Dawkins: "If you discovered a really impressive fine-tuning ... I think you'd really be left with only two explanations: a benevolent designer or a multiverse."

Weinberg went on to clarify that invoking a benevolent designer does not count as a genuine explanation, but I was intrigued by his either/or scenario. Is that really our only choice? Supernatural creator or parallel worlds?

It is according to an article in ... *Discover* magazine. "Short of invoking a benevolent creator, many physicists see only one possible explanation," writes journalist Tim Folger. "Our universe may be but one of perhaps infinitely many universes in an inconceivably vast multiverse." Folger quotes cosmologist Bernard Carr: "If you don't want God, you'd better have a multiverse."

There are plenty of reasons to take the multiverse seriously. Three key theories—quantum mechanics, cosmic inflation and string theory—all converge on the idea. But the reason physicists talk about the multiverse as an alternative to God is because it helps explain why the universe is so bio-friendly. From the strength of gravity to the mass of a proton, it's as if the universe were designed just for us. If, however, there are an infinite number of universes—with physical constants that vary from one to the next—our cosy neighbourhood isn't only possible, it's inevitable.[30]

Physicist Lee Smolin and Harvard law professor Roberto Unger have this to say about that, however:

> The problem with theories that include hidden dimensions and alternate universes, he says, is that they are not theories at all but allegories. There is no way to test them with any experiments or observations. String theory cannot be made to work in a world of only four dimensions. In response, string theorists posited the existence of seven extra dimensions that are hidden from us. Of course, no one has observed these extra dimensions of space, and worse, it is not clear that such an observation is possible. The equations of string theory predict that there are an unimaginable number of different possibilities for how those dimensions are configured—on the order of 10 to the 500th

---

[30] Amanda Gefter, *NewScientist*, 6 Dec 2008, page 48

power. It would take more time than has so far elapsed since the Big Bang just to count them all.

The experimental basis for a multiverse theory is equally shaky. None of the other universes that crop up could ever be seen because the space between us and them would be expanding at faster-than-light speed.

Neither string theory nor the multiverse theory explain nature's mysteries so much as explain them away, Unger concludes. "When we imagine our universe to be just one out of a multitude of possible worlds, we devalue this world, the one we see, the one we should be trying to explain," he says. "The scientist should treasure the riddles he can't solve, not explain them away at the outset."

Unger and Smolin want to shift the emphasis in physics away from these possible worlds and back to the one real world—our world, which is saturated with time. They urge their colleagues to abandon the search for timeless truths like string theory.

More broadly, they argue that physics should refrain from spinning any theories that require the existence of things that could never be disproved, such as multiverses.[31]

Furthermore, in a sign of the dynamism of science, it seems as though even the multiverse does not solve the problem of the original origin. This from New Scientist in January of 2012:

> While many of us may be OK with the idea of the big bang simply starting everything, physicists, including Hawking, tend to shy away from cosmic genesis. "A point of creation would be a place where science broke down. One would have to appeal to religion and the hand of God," Hawking told the meeting, at the University of Cambridge, in a pre-recorded speech.
>
> For a while it looked like it might be possible to dodge this problem, by relying on models such as an eternally inflating or cyclic universe, both of which seemed to continue infinitely in the past as well as the future. Perhaps surprisingly, these were also both compatible with the big bang, the idea that the universe most likely burst forth from an extremely dense, hot state about 13.7 billion years ago.
>
> However, as cosmologist Alexander Vilenkin of Tufts University in Boston explained last week, that hope has been gradually fading and may

---

[31] http://discovermagazine.com/2010/apr/10-is-search-for-immutable-laws-of-nature-wild-goose-chase/

now be dead. He showed that all these theories still demand a beginning.[32]

And finally, four, God made the original observation (assuming God exists) and collapsed the wave function, causing the universe to pop into being and to exist continually. That creates another question, though. If God is the observer, then why is the wave function not collapsed for humans now? Not surprisingly, there is no answer and no discussion of this issue in science, not even a consideration of it.

So I'll have to make up an answer: God was the original and ongoing observer until humans arrived on the scene, whereupon he abrogated that role to us and we became the observers. It is the only option that is consistent with our universe-observer problem, and theologically it may suggest that the way we are made in God's image is that we are now the observers.

It also solves another intriguing issue raised by at least one film, *What the Bleep Do We Know?*, which states firmly and absolutely falsely that we can control the outcome of any observation, that we can in fact choose the reality we get. We cannot.[33] Thus we are absolutely the arbiters of whether or not reality exists, and absolutely powerless to determine the nature of that reality. I will suggest, outside of science, that this is what ensures that we are not God: God can control the outcome of the observation, and we cannot. Not only is the principal message of scripture that God is God, and we are not, but a significant message in nature is the same. You gotta admire the confluence.

And so we have the Relativistic God, outside of time and space, and the Quantum God, the God who can be everywhere at once, who can go from here to there instantaneously, who can spin matter out of energy, complex forms out of the quantum, and a universe out of nothing at all, the creator of time and space, the God who is God of the largest and the smallest, the God who took the smallest of all possible things, the Singularity, and made the largest of all

---

[32] **Why physicists can't avoid a creation event,** New Scientist, 11 January 2012 by Lisa Grossman

[33] From Dr. Jeffrey Satinover in response to my email to him on this question, 21 June 2005. Dr. Satinover (Laboratoire de Physique de la Matière Condensée Chambre 2.08, Centre National de la Recherche Scientifique Université de Nice - Sophia Antipolis) was a featured scientist in the film: "The film is pretty fuzzy on this point and a number of closely related ones. It doesn't exactly say that in QM the observer controls which eigenvector of a superposition is selected, but for all practical purposes it leaves the viewer with the impression that it's possible to do something like that in everyday life and this arises out of QM. Of course, the former is partially true—you can move your legs, an example of mind controlling matter which has yet to be explained adequately by any one, but if a locomotive is bearing down on you, you'd better use this everyday miracle to get off the tracks, and don't expect that you can create a reality in which your thinking the locomotive will stop will make it. But you're right, no such deliberate selection is possible by the mere act of observation per se. But then, the movie's representation of state vectors and superpositions in QM is incorrect as well, setting up this confusion."

possible things, the universe itself. He did so in a tiny fraction of a second, cloaking the original moments in inaccessible mystery, but allowing us to know much of what happened via the existence of the forces of nature, the laws of physics, the evidence that lurks almost unseen, almost unknowable, but not quite.

He is the God for whom the extraordinary became the ordinary, and for whom the extraordinary is hidden deep within the ordinary, and though those two phrases and indeed much of this paragraph sound very much like theology, they are also just purely quantum. Singularity was just potential, as are each of us: quantum us in the hands of a quantum God, real and transcendent because of his love for us, unbelievably tiny and insignificant without it.

Reductionists would have us believe that because there is not much to us, there is nothing to us at all, but the evidence of science itself tells us that it is the apparently tiny and insignificant that transform the universe from nothing into everything. It seems that though the universe is full of tiny things, there is nothing that is insignificant.

But as we will see, it is only when the tiny things interact on a larger scale that significance emerges. And perhaps the most significant things of all are the observers.

*Glossary of Terms as they are alluded to in Chapter Five

The **Anthropic Principle** – Physicist Brandon Carter in the '70s, preceded by evolutionary biologist Alfred Russel Wallace in 1904 and Robert Dicke in 1961, looked around at the parameters in the universe necessary for life to exist and decided that they were improbable enough that it bore investigating. His investigations caused him to announce in a symposium in 1973 that humans, or more specifically life in general, occupied a special place in space and time. From Wikipedia: "The phrase 'anthropic principle'" first appeared in Brandon Carter's contribution to a 1973 Kraków symposium honouring Copernicus's 500th birthday. Carter, a theoretical astrophysicist, articulated the Anthropic Principle in reaction to the Copernican Principle, which states that humans do not occupy a privileged position (in time as well as space) in the Universe. As Carter said: 'Although our situation is not necessarily central, it is inevitably privileged to some extent.'" [34]

Wallace wrote in 1904, "Such a vast and complex universe as that which we know exists around us, may have been absolutely required ... in order to produce a world that should be precisely adapted in every detail for the orderly development of life culminating in man."[35]

In 1957, Robert Dicke wrote: "The age of the Universe 'now' is not random but conditioned by biological factors ... [changes in the values of the fundamental constants of physics] would preclude the existence of man to consider the problem."[36]

Since that time, it has become a controversial and yet hard-to-debunk principle in physics – the universe seems to have exactly the right set of scientific laws and realities to produce and support life.

One part of the AP that is not as often discussed is the need for an intelligent observer to cause reality to come into being – the Copenhagen, or standard Interpretation of Quantum Physics. Princeton Physicist John Wheeler was the leading proponent of what he called the Participatory AP.

Other parts include many constants and values found in nature that cause it to appear "fine-tuned" for life, and perhaps even for human life. For information on these constants and values, visit Hugh Ross' website, www.reasons.org/fine-tuning-life-universe.

Wikipedia gives a well-balanced exploration of the substance and controversial nature of the AP.

---

[34] http://en.wikipedia.org/wiki/Anthropic_principle

[35] ibid

[36] ibid

Chapter 6

Good Parking Spots, Hot Wives, and Great Hair

We've spent some time talking about Relativity and Quantum Mechanics, which is not about your relatives who are tiny mechanics. What Relativity has done for us is from within science to eliminate the possibility of the universe being infinitely old, and it has done this via Big Bang, that primal moment when everything that would ever be anything became something. What QM has done for us is to disabuse us of the notion that the universe is predetermined as a history and a timeline, that is, that everything is caused by something in a definitive and infinitely describable way such that free will vanishes as an option. Putting infinity together with determinism, and you have a formula for a universe that doesn't need God, or gods. Given enough time and enough particles bouncing off each other with predetermined velocities and locations, and anything can happen, so that everything becomes a big accident of time and effects. I personally refuse to believe that chocolate is a big accident of anything, but that's just my personal theology.

But now we haven't had enough time for that or anything else to have happened, thanks to Big Bang, and besides, the universe is put together in a far different way than we would ever have assumed. It is not purely deterministic.

And it's neither purely mechanistic nor reductionistic anymore, though we will deal with each of those further. At the quantum level, things are not predictable—they are probabilistic, and the probabilities can be extraordinarily precisely calculated (I've heard it described by Richard Dawkins as the equivalent of being able to predict the width of North America to a precision of the width of a human hair), but things that happen all the time at the quantum level are counterintuitive and baffling. The universe is not purely mechanistic on the quantum level, and there is no line dividing the quantum from the rest of the world.[37]

As far as reductionism goes, one of its two tenets is that the smaller the parts we can reduce something to, the better we will understand it. But now we know that at the quantum level, not only do we not understand things better, we don't understand things at all.

Already we have slain the dragon—the four horsemen of scientific atheism are dead. We should be happy.

---

[37] "Where the boundary is between the quantum and classical worlds, no one really knows," says NIST guest researcher John Jost, a graduate student at the University of Colorado at Boulder. www.sciencedaily.com/releases/2009/06/090603131429.htm

Alas, some of us are not happy at all. Some are unhappy because they were expecting another assault on Big Bang and support added for a 6000-year-old earth, universe and cosmology. Others also want a six-day creation story.

I'm going to upset your apple carts in a much more disturbing way than those. First, though, let me throw you a bone.

I can give you a 6000-year creation cosmology from science. Quantum Mechanics, as we read above, allows for almost anything to pop into existence out of nothing, including a universe, which we know to be true from Big Bang at the very least. Now, is it possible or likely for a universe to have popped into existence 6000 years ago, fully formed and functioning? Though I run the risk of aggravating a lot of people, I would have to say that yes, it is possible, and is actually more likely than Big Bang itself. After all, Big Bang produced a universe that was almost perfect, with almost zero entropy, an extremely unlikely arrival, so since the universe of 6000 years ago had a lot more entropy in it, it seems like an easier solution. So it seems to me that yes, it's possible.

I don't think it happened that way, though, because if it did, then we can't have a 6-day creation story, and that story, unlike the 6000-year creation cosmology, is Biblical. Relativity very comfortably allows for both a 6-day creation story and a 13.7-billion year creation cosmology, as demonstrated by physicist Gerald Schroeder in *"The Science of God"* and as we talked about in *Life, the Universe, and Everything*. Space-time dilation means that millions or billions of years and one day can be exactly the same. Time is a relative sort of thing. Always has been. No worries. Well, not exactly *always*, since *always* is a time word, but still.

Let me also add a bit of evangelistic advice, just for free. Since a 6000-year creation cosmology is extrabiblical, continuing to believe it is not important enough to destroy your witness for Christ over. It used to be that people of faith thought that the universe rotated around the earth, and it was just as important for those folks to believe that as it is for some of us to hold onto 6000 years of history. They felt that if anyone tried to deny the truth of a geocentric universe, the entire validity of the Bible would be destroyed. People were tortured and killed for claiming anything different.

Didn't work out that way. None of us believe in a geocentric universe. It has no impact on our belief in Christ. It's gone, never to return, and we are still here with our faith intact.

Same thing is true about the flat earth. It was flat. You could tell by looking. We could even find verses in scripture that clearly indicated that the earth was flat. It would be blasphemy and heresy to suggest that it was not.

But the earth is round, and our faith is real and untainted. Our faith was not destroyed by the discovery that the world is not flat.

Thus will it be for a 6000-year creation cosmology. Many will feel that if the apparent truth of Genesis 1 is lost, then the entirety of the Gospel message will be imperiled. If you can't believe Genesis 1, or so it is said, then how can you believe anything else? It's either all true, or none of it is true.

But there are many marvelous believers who do not believe in a 6000-year creation story, people of great faith in Christ who nonetheless believe in Big Bang as the way that God created the universe out of nothing. For them, it is not a challenge to their faith, no more than a geocentric universe or a flat earth would be. And their witness to people who believe that science is true and that religion is ignorant is far more powerful because of Big Bang. Remember that Big Bang was rejected by the great men of science because it sounded far too much like what we were saying that our God had done. *They* knew that it sounded like Genesis 1. So why don't we?

So do you want people to believe in Jesus, or to disbelieve in Big Bang? What is *your* gospel message?

We have been quick to point fingers at science for claiming truth and then changing it as the evidence changes, but as we have said, we as believers have been dragged into an understanding of God and the universe that will range from mildly deficient to radically delusional, but unlike science, we are loathe to change our understanding of our faith and of our God as evidence changes. Though science can be a bit arrogant in staking out its truth territory, and can also be extremely reluctant to acknowledge that its old truth is now obsolete, still it is the glory of science that it does move on. Religion cannot easily make such a claim.

Science makes progress via insults, calumny, slander, libel, and an occasional fistfight, but ultimately the next road on the path to truth is taken. Religions change via shunnings, ostracisms, wars, inquisitions, crusades, excommunications, stake burnings, cross burnings, and crucifixions, and then the original form of the faith generally doesn't change at all, but has learned to come to angry and resentful terms with whatever the new form happens to be. It must be admitted that sometimes the new form is not really new, but the original form of the corrupted original, and sometimes the new form is really new and probably heretical. These things never surprise God, but we often times seem to think that he's not paying close enough attention, and we need to take the appropriate steps to protect him in his age and senility.

It does depend on whether or not the heresy is actually heretical, of course.

Now let's really getting into some serious boat-rockin'. Here is the accusation:

We have let Determinism, Mechanism, and Reductionism define God for us. I'm not sure why, though I think it all crept in gradually over time out of 1) a desire rooted in intellectual insecurity and defensiveness to be metaphysically consonant with science and its precepts, or 2) incipient individualism which in turn migrated in from humanism, also known as the archenemy of faith, secular humanism. But it is intriguing that out of the four significant precepts of Newtonian science that have continued to define the way we pursue science in the modern age, we have denied the one that offers the most powerful evidence of God to be found in nature (that is, that Big Bang has replaced infinity with a finite universe) and blissfully and unconsciously accepted the three that are still a challenge to God's existence.

We'll hold off on Mechanism and Reductionism for several more chapters, and deal now with Determinism.

What Determinism says about the structure of the universe is that everything is predetermined. What many of us believe about life as believers is that God has predetermined everything for us.

We have taken a handful of verses and turned them into a theology of Christian Determinism. To wit:

> "And we know that in all things God works for the good of those who love him, who have been called according to his purpose. For those God foreknew he also predestined to be conformed to the likeness of his Son, that he might be the firstborn among many brothers. And those he predestined, he also called; those he called, he also justified; those he justified, he also glorified."[38]

Our understanding of our *cher frere* Jean Calvin of Geneva is that he used this to take away the need or even the possibility of having made a free will decision to follow Christ—everything has been predetermined for us. That thought in turn has warped quite thoroughly our understanding of how faith gets lived out. Though I admire Bill Bright and Campus Crusade, he and the organization use a phrase that typifies this as a concept—"God has a wonderful plan for your life." I believe this to be bad theology and bad way to live a life in Christ.

We have somehow evolved an understanding that each moment, each second of our lives has been mapped out for us in advance. God has planned every step along the way out to the smallest of moments and the tiniest of events. The catch? He's not telling you what it is. You have to figure it out yourself. It's like

---

[38] Romans 8:28-30, NIV

this massive, deadly cosmic video game where you have to shoot the bad guys and find the secret weapons and clues along the way, only you get no start-again option.

Further, he has planned your existence since the beginning of time, which we now know actually has a beginning, and the existence of everyone who has ever lived and will ever lived.

Listen to Paul Davies writing about Laplace, and see how similar it sounds:

> Laplace pointed out that if a super-intelligent demon knew at one instant the position and motion of every particle in the universe, and the forces acting between them, the demon could do a massive calculation and predict the future in every detail, including the emergence of life and the behaviour of every human being. This startling conclusion remains an unstated act of faith among many scientists.[39]

It remains an act of faith among people of faith as well. Since God knows all and sees all, he must plan all.

One has to admit how comforting this is. God has it all planned out, and all we have to do is be faithful people of prayer to discover his direction and plan. Through prayer, fasting, purity, spiritual discipline, Bible study, and the wise counsel of Godly men and women, we'll find his plan and direction for our lives and fulfill that plan to the glory of his kingdom.

Nice story. Bad theology.

Let's remind ourselves that what determinism did was to remove free will from the picture, and thus what Quantum Mechanics does is to restore the potential and possibility for free will decisions to be made. If God has predetermined everything, then once again, free will evaporates. Where we might consider free will just as the source of sin, as indeed it is, free will is also about love, commitment, and choices made day-by-day, moment-by-moment. If God has a predetermined plan for each of us, and if we define free will as being that which leads to sin, then our only choices are to find God's mysterious and hidden path for our lives, or to wander unwittingly into sin, not from any rebellion or refusal to follow God, but simply from an inability to figure it out.

God has given us free will. That is the story of the Garden and the Fall, and it is the story of salvation (ignoring the Calvinist problem for the moment). At some level, we all believe that the choice to follow Christ is exactly that, a

---

[39] Paul Davies, New Scientist Magazine, 5 March 05

choice. Can we then believe that free will ceases to apply after we have made a decision for faith, except where we choose to rebel? I don't think so.

So follow this to its logical conclusion. Free will is a gift from God, one that we abuse to bad ends and use to good ends. So how does this play out in the stories of our lives? Do we each have one correct path to follow, distracted at every turn by false hints and rabbit trails, terrified that somehow we will miss God's plan for our lives?

In a word, no, and it's pretty simple to see in three easy steps.

One. We are all called. It seems that we have developed a theology of "call" that is primarily geographical as well as occupational. God is supposed to "call" people to specific ministries in specific locations. Missionaries get to go to cool and scary places which God will tell them about very precisely. The rest of us have to stay closer to familiar haunts, but whenever an opportunity for ministry presents itself, we have to pray about it to see whether or not God has "called" us to it.

Let's say it again—we are all called, and it has nothing to do with occupation or geography. Jesus was alarmingly specific: "go and make disciples of all nations, baptizing them in the name of the Father and of the Son and of the Holy Spirit, and teaching them to obey everything I have commanded you" from Matthew 28:19-20 (NIV). That's not just for some of us. It has nothing to do with geography. It's for all of us, everywhere, all the time.

We are all called to build the kingdom, to be witnesses for the Gospel in every job that we do, every relationship that we have, every place we live, even if we never leave the first place, even if we live in hundreds of places. And we are to teach them to follow his commands—feed the hungry, clothe the naked, visit the sick and the prisoners. You know the drill. Nobody's exempt. Everybody gets a call, and that's it. Build the kingdom of God. No exceptions.

Two. We each have gifts, experiences, talents and skills, knowledge, wisdom and inclinations that will best serve the call. For example, I am called to be a witness, and I am good with kids. So my call will be best used if I work with kids—teaching, coaching, youth grouping, that kind of thing. I might have other things I do well—skiing, for one. So my wife and I volunteered at a ski resort, we got to be witnesses in our dealings with our fellow volunteers, and we got to help those who need help on the slopes, the injured, lost, separated from their parents, and so on. I try to put my skills into God's hands to be used to help build his kingdom. I might also get to, or am forced to, learn new skills, not getting to rest comfortably where I am, but to be challenged to be more for the kingdom.

And that leads to *Three*. God wants most for me to be dependent on him, to place my faith moment by moment in him, and not to rely solely on my own abilities and strengths. Paul wrote that God wanted to use him where he was weak:

> To keep me from becoming conceited because of these surpassingly great revelations, there was given me a thorn in my flesh, a messenger of Satan, to torment me. Three times I pleaded with the Lord to take it away from me. But he said to me, 'My grace is sufficient for you, for my power is made perfect in weakness.' Therefore I will boast all the more gladly about my weaknesses, so that Christ's power may rest on me.[40]

So how do I use my skills and talents (where I am strong) in such a way as to force faith in and dependence on God? I take risks in the faith, and the nature and scope of those risks will stretch me, if I am willing and bold enough to be stretched. God will use us where we are, even if we refuse to leave our comfort zones, but it is harder for us to have strong faith if we are not challenged by the unknown.

So if you want to go to Africa, take off. By and large, God is not calling most missionaries to specific locations, even the vast majority of missionaries. I mean, really. Have you seen the size of the universe relative to the size of Earth? And you think God is all into sending you to Africa or Asia? Please.

God is into using you wherever you are. You can't make a wrong geographical decision. It's not as though God is "calling you" to Ouagadougou and you refuse to go, and then he pouts and refuses to use you in Okefenokee, and your life is wasted. He will use you, if you are willing, no matter where you are. But he may stretch you more in Ouagadougou, and the change and growth you will experience will transform you into somebody you likely never would have become in Okefenokee. That's in Florida, by the way. Ouagadougou is in Burkina Faso, which is, in turn, Africa. I just like saying Ouagadougou.

That's free will. You get to choose where you go and what you do with your life. For some, that's terrifying. We might find it vastly more comforting to believe that God has it all planned out, since his plans for us are far better than our own. And God does have a plan, just not one for your life. He has a plan for all of us. Build the kingdom. Use your gifts. Take some risks in faith. How you do these things is not predetermined nor planned out. It's your choice.

Scary? Maybe. But it's also freeing—apart from falling into sin itself, you can't make a mistake. There are no guarantees that it will work out the way you might have wanted it to. You might get out of a boat and get speared to death

---

[40] 2 Corinthians 12:7-9, New International Version

by frightened natives in the first five minutes after you arrive. You might get arrested and vanish into a camp somewhere, never to be seen again. You might get hung or shot or beaten or tortured. Or worse, you might get ignored. The results are God's, but the path is yours to choose. Choose wisely.

And remember the quantum: all paths exist until one is chosen, and then all the rest vanish. You have observed your own reality into existence. God gives you the power to make the choice, but you have no control over the outcome. Well, at this level, at the macro level, you have some control, some input, some free will choices and decisions to make that will define the way things develop. But as we will see in the next few chapters, sometimes the Butterfly wins.

Just to clarify for some of you who are jumping and down and spitting with anger and frustration, am I saying that God does not call people? No, I can't put God in a box and tell him what to do. But I am saying that everyone is called, not just the few, and we are all called to the same thing wherever we are. Does God call someone in a special way every now and then? Well, he did in the Bible, so I'm guessing that the answer is yes. Remember, though; every call he issued in the Bible had one purpose—building the kingdom.

So has he called every pastor and missionary into service? Does he have a plan for the type of house you own, or the bigger house you want to own, or the car you drive or the clothes you buy? Does he have one person for you to marry, the precise number of children you are supposed to have? Has he chosen a college or a career for you? Do you live in the town you live in because God has put you there? Has he micromanaged your life, and does he and will he continue to do so?

No. Free will is free will. The universe has not been on a predetermined path for 13.7 billion years to provide you with a better parking spot, a hot wife, or great hair. Those are your choices within the constraints of culture, history, and the state of being human. Now, use them for the glory of God and the building of the kingdom. Feed the hungry, clothe the naked, visit the sick and imprisoned, care for the widows and orphans. Fear wealth. Love God, and love everybody else. Forgive seven times seventy. Stay away from judging and condemnation, from intolerance and hatred. Be generous and give things and money away. Be merciful and full of grace. Don't be right; live right. Don't worry so much about truth; worry about grace. Truth tends to take care of itself over time. Grace is your job.

Be the fractal Jesus.

We'll talk about that soon.

Chapter 7

Chaos Out of Order

In the interest of being able to fit the title on the front of the book, I neglected to mention that we were also going to be talking about the Chaotic God and the Complex God, and rather than scare you off, I waited until right now to mention it, suspecting that it is far more likely that you have actually bought the book by now instead of reading it for free with coffee in a bookstore the way my daughter does.

Most books would have titled this chapter a bit differently, too: same words, different order; that is, if we are going to talk about God, then we are going to talk about God bringing order out of chaos and blah blah blah. We'll do that in a minute, but you can't do that unless you talk about chaos coming out of order first. Perhaps we should explain. We're not just trying to be cute here—just shattering paradigms.

A mechanistic universe is, as we have said, a universe that is alleged to run like clockwork. Wind it up, let it go, except of course in an infinite universe, no one has to wind it up. We've already seen that we don't have an infinite universe, and that the clock had to have been wound up in a quantum sort of way (neither wound nor not wound, would be the Schroedinger's Cat explanation of that, which doesn't help even a little bit).

So we already have a problem with a mechanistic universe, but let's skip that part of the problem and go to the core of the issue. A mechanistic universe is predictable, because machines are predictable. Machines do what machines are designed to do, unless they are broken, but that's a predictable part of machineness, especially in the computer age. Truth is, machines are designed to break so that you will have to buy new machines—planned obsolescence is what made the US car industry the stellar industry that it was—so in fact machines still do exactly what they are designed to do, even if they are not doing what you thought they were supposed to do when you naïvely bought them in the first place.

Chaos Theory puts an end to predictability, and an end to a purely mechanistic universe. We also have the problem of entropy to discuss, but that will appear presently. For now, let's talk Chaos.

Chaos Theory, which essentially appeared as a new field of science courtesy of Ed Lorenz out of MIT in 1961, tells us that there are too many things going on at once for things to be predictable, and the more interesting things are, the more unpredictable they are. Science traditionally wants to try to remove all outside influences from any experimental situation in order to ensure predictability, and where that works pretty well to give us the ability to make predictions under idealized circumstances, life hardly ever gives us the ideal.

For example, let's assume that space is empty. Wait, can't do that. Space is not empty. Little bits of seething virtual particles all around.

OK, let's assume that we have particles. Wait, can't do that. They aren't really particles.

Let's assume waves. Nope.

Let's assume time moves in one direction. Ah, well, you know, most of the time, except for those particles.

Let's assume the laws of physics work everywhere in the universe. That's not bad, except for in black hole singularities, where they don't work any more, or early inside Big Bang, where we didn't have laws yet, or at the quantum level, where relativity and quantum mechanics, the two finest and most predictive laws known to man, are incompatible.

Can't we just talk about the weather? Hah! You wish.

Let's talk about what might be the greatest example of unpredictability in weather in our times, the one thing we didn't write about in the last book because it sort of didn't occur to us at the time, and that would be: Global Warming, now being called Climate Change to avoid confusion.

Allow me to fly in the face of chaotic unpredictability to make the prediction that you, the readers, just divided yourselves into two groups—those who believe in Climate Change, and those who don't, that is, two groups who tend as a rule to consider everybody in the other group a raving lunatic.

Group One: Climate Change and its causes are well established by overwhelming scientific evidence, all the scientists believe it, and those who deny its reality are either ignorant religious zealots who don't believe anything is true in science or rich fat-cat capitalists who don't want to stop making profits for single second even if the fate of the entire world is at stake.

Group Two: Things are clearly getting warmer, but establishing a causal link between "things getting warmer" and "it's all our fault" has hardly been established by the evidence in any sense, not all the scientists believe it, but the ones who disagree have been intimidated by the scientific community into keeping quiet about it, except for a few who have been courageous enough to speak out, only to be pilloried on the altar of scientific fanaticism, and besides, "things getting warmer" cannot be said with any certainty to be either a long-term or short-term weather anomaly, a major trend or a minor blip.

Both groups are now busily trying to analyze the two paragraphs above to see if they can figure out my bias, and then stop reading because I am either 1) an idiot or 2) an idiot. And if I claim that I don't have a bias, or if I don't actually have a bias, then I am 1) an idiot or 2) an idiot.

Here's what Chaos Theory says about weather: it's fundamentally unpredictable. We can predict about 3-4 days out, but then only if there's not much change. Beyond that, we can't really make predictions that have any real chance of coming true unless things just happen not to change very much. But introduce any small perturbations into the system, and even inside of those 3-4 days, the predictions can go badly wrong.

Chaos tells us that there are far too many tiny variables for us to be able to know about and anticipate in any dynamic system like weather (or others like economics, genetics, or any other field of science). I have read that the difference between rain and no rain is a half degree of temperature variation. Science made an assumption that if you could just know enough information about any set of circumstances, then you could make accurate predictions for the future—remember Laplace's contention? Everything is predetermined, everything is predictable.

But QM has told us that determinism doesn't hold at the quantum level because you can't know what you need to know. Now Chaos is telling us that you can't know what you need to know at the largest levels.

Let's look at Climate Change from both sides, but from the perspective of Chaos Theory.

Remembering the fundamentals of Chaos, let's see if we find any evidence. The evidence for Global Warming is undeniable, or at least for global warming —things are getter warmer. Some would want to look at this in an overly simplistic way, expecting everything to be getting warmer all at once everywhere, but weather doesn't work that way. If there are over-warming trends, they will manifest themselves in complex and hard-to-predict sorts of ways.

But let's start with the basics—causation. The theory is that excess carbon dioxide in the atmosphere is causing the earth to heat up via what is called the "greenhouse effect." As Time Magazine wrote about it in a 2006 cover story,

> As a tiny component of our atmosphere, carbon dioxide helped warm Earth to comfort levels we are all used to. But too much of it does an awful lot of damage. The gas represents just a few hundred parts per million (p.p.m.) in the overall air blanket, but they're powerful parts because they allow sunlight to stream in but prevent much of the heat from radiating back out. During the last ice age, the atmosphere's CO^2 concentration was just 180 p.p.m., putting Earth into a deep freeze.

After the glaciers retreated but before the dawn of the modern era, the total had risen to a comfortable 280 p.p.m. In just the past century and a half, we have pushed the level to 381 p.p.m., and we're feeling the effects. Of the 20 hottest years on record, 19 occurred in the 1980s or later. According to NASA scientists, 2005 was one of the hottest years in more than a century.[41]

That trend has continued through 2008, with each year being a hotter year than the norm would allow for.

This is beautifully and terrifyingly Chaotic—a *one percent of one percent* change in the chemistry of the atmosphere may have precipitated this threat to life itself on the planet. As Time says later in the article, "We're finally coming to appreciate the knife-blade margins within which life can thrive."[42] The language is pure Chaos:

> What few people reckoned on was that global climate systems are booby-trapped with *tipping points* and *feedback loops*, thresholds past which the slow creep of environmental decay gives way to *sudden and self-perpetuating collapse*. Pump enough CO^2 into the sky, and that last part per million of greenhouse gas behaves like the 212th degree Fahrenheit that turns a pot of hot water into a plume of billowing steam.[43]

Tipping points and feedback loops that lead to sudden collapse—nothing but Chaos.

That's what Chaos is all about—a butterfly effect where tiny, immeasurable changes in a system (like the tiny flapping of a butterfly's wing...) gradually build up over time until the system itself collapses (...causing something huge like a hurricane), and the collapse is sudden and essentially unpredictable, if not unexpected entirely. It's not that the ice caps in Greenland and Antarctica gradually melt away over dozens or hundreds of years—it's that they may suddenly slide into the ocean in a matter of days or even hours.

Further, "Ocean waters have warmed by a full degree Fahrenheit since 1970, and warmer water is like rocket fuel for typhoons and hurricanes. Two studies last year found that in the past 35 years the number of Category 4 and 5 hurricanes worldwide has doubled while the wind speed and duration of all

---

[41] *Time Magazine*, 3 April 2006, Special Report, Global Warming
[42] Ibid.
[43] Ibid.

hurricanes has jumped 50%."[44] Again, waters have warmed by . . . one degree. It doesn't seem like much, but it seems that a one degree temperature rise is enough to change the strength and duration of hurricanes worldwide. Tiny variations, tiny changes in initial conditions, and a huge impact on the outcome.

The changes trigger feedback loops that have impacts of their own—drier conditions mean more forest fires, which mean more carbon in the air. Melting permafrost means more carbon in the air. Warmer water expands, starting to flood coastal areas, and water absorbs heat where ice reflects it, so with less ice and more water, more heat is absorbed and the changes accelerate. Small changes (the butterfly) become a runaway train (the hurricane) that eventually reaches a point where it can't be stopped.

And so the fear that we are losing control of our planet, and the changes will be life-threatening to plants and animals driven uphill by the heat and off the coastlines by the rising seas, and ultimately life-threatening to Bangladeshis and Londoners and New Yorkers and Floridians and low-lying island dwellers and coastal dwellers worldwide.

Now is the moment to begin our transition to the other side, but intriguingly, we'll be able to use arguments from the pro-Climate Change side to make that transition:

From *Science Daily*, in the article "Stronger Evidence For Human Origin Of Global Warming":

> A recent statistical analysis strengthens evidence that human activities are causing world temperatures to rise. Most climate change scientists model Earth systems from the ground up, attempting to account for all climate driving forces. *Unfortunately, small changes in the models can lead to a broad range of outcomes, inviting debate over the actual causes of climate change.*[45] (italics mine)

And here we begin to see the difficulty inherent in the debate: small changes in data entered into the computer models use to model climate change drastically alter the outcome, rendering climate change radically unpredictable. As much as causation seems established, it is only via computer models that the evidence for causation has been established, and those models are struck senseless in the face of tiny variations in the data.

---

[44] Ibid.
[45] Sciencedaily.com, Stronger Evidence For Human Origin Of Global Warming, 1 Aug 2007

And again from the very next day: *Science Daily,* "Synchronized Chaos: Mechanisms For Major Climate Shifts":

> In the mid-1970s, a climate shift cooled sea surface temperatures in the central Pacific Ocean and warmed the coast of western North America, bringing long-range changes to the northern hemisphere. After this climate shift waned, an era of frequent of *El Niños* and rising global temperatures began. *Understanding the mechanisms driving such climate variability is difficult because unraveling causal connections that lead to chaotic climate behavior is complicated.*[46] (italics mine)

And from the Ludwig von Mises Institute in Vienna:

> Carbon dioxide is a greenhouse gas, proved in a laboratory a century ago. Global warming has been occurring for a century and concentrations of atmospheric carbon have been rising for a century. Correlation is not causation, but in a rough sense it looked like a fit. Ice core data allowed us to measure temperature and atmospheric carbon going back hundreds of thousands of years, through several dramatic global warming and cooling events. To the temporal resolution then available (data points more than a thousand years apart), atmospheric carbon and temperature moved in lockstep: they rose and fell together. There were no other credible causes of global warming.
>
> Better data shows that from 1940 to 1975 the earth cooled while atmospheric carbon increased. That 35 year non-correlation might eventually be explained by global dimming, only discovered in about 2003. The temporal resolution of the ice core data improved. By 2004 we knew that in past warming events, the temperature increases generally started about 800 years before the rises in atmospheric carbon. Causality does not run in the direction assumed in 1999—it runs the opposite way...
>
> *There is now no observational evidence that global warming is caused by carbon emissions* (italics mine). You would think that in over 20 years of intense investigation we would have found something. The only current "evidence" for blaming carbon emissions are scientific models (and the fact that there are few contradictory observations). Historically, science has not progressed by calculations and models, but by repeatable observations. None of the new evidence actually says that carbon

---

[46] Ibid, 2 Aug 2007

emissions are definitely not the cause of global warming. After 2000 the case against carbon emissions gradually got weaker. Future evidence might strengthen or further weaken it. At what stage of the weakening should the science community alert the political system that carbon emissions might not be the main cause of global warming?[47]

More confusion? *ScienceDaily,* "Arctic Ocean Circulation Does An About-Face":

> A team of NASA and university scientists has detected an ongoing reversal in Arctic Ocean circulation triggered by atmospheric circulation changes that vary on decade-long time scales. The results suggest not all the large changes seen in Arctic climate in recent years are a result of long-term trends associated with global warming.[48]

And still more, from National Public Radio:

> Some 3,000 scientific robots that are plying the ocean have sent home a puzzling message. These diving instruments suggest that the oceans have not warmed up at all over the past four or five years. That could mean global warming has taken a breather. Or it could mean scientists aren't quite understanding what their robots are telling them.[49]

Why stop now? "Scientists Debate The Accuracy Of Al Gore's Documentary 'An Inconvenient Truth'":

> Roy Spencer from the University of Alabama: In his view, the film's main omission is that while humans are almost certainly responsible for global warming, there are other natural causes of climate variability which the film does not address. In his opinion, the real inconvenient truth is that science has no idea how much of recent warming is natural versus the result of human activities.

---

[47] David Evans, *I Was On the Global Warming Gravy Train*, Ludwig von Mises Institute, http://mises.org/story/2571
[48] *ScienceDaily Nov. 14, 2007*
[49] National Public Radio: *Morning Edition*, March 19, 2008

And finally: in *Science Daily*, "Global Warming Has Little Impact In Tropical Storm And Hurricane Numbers, NOAA Reports":

> This new study suggests that in the Atlantic basin, global warming from increasing greenhouse gases will have little impact, or perhaps cause some decrease, in tropical storm and hurricane numbers.[50]

What you will note now is that I am not going through the standard responses of the anti-Climate Change side of the debate, because they only reinforce what Chaos is telling us about Climate Change in the pages above. Though it seems likely or at least reasonable that human contributions to the atmosphere in terms of carbon emissions are in large part responsible for Climate Change, there is literally no way to know for sure. The time spans are too large, the variables too tiny and varied, the tolerances and parameters too hard to control, and since all of the predictions for the future are coming from computer models, we are forced to remember that it was tiny variations in data input that led Ed Lorenz at MIT to discover and develop Chaos Theory as a field of human inquiry.

For some of us, this will be terrifying, for others, reassuring. For all of us, it will stand as a monumental example of the limitations of human reason in trying to understand the vagaries of mother nature. Weather is, and always will be, fundamentally unpredictable, and we may never know what is causing Climate Change, though we will certainly know, after the fact, whether it is a threat to life on the planet or just a short-term hiccup. I'm thinking we probably ought to do something, just in case, but that's just me.

The question remains, though: what does all of this have to say about God? I'd very much like to be unpredictable here and not deal with it, but in this case, you can safely predict that we will talk about it. But you may not be able to predict what we might say. Ah, Chaos.

---

[50] *ScienceDaily*, May 20, 2008

Chapter 8

Our God is an Awesomely Chaotic God

The Butterfly Effect tells us that sometimes something as small as the flapping of a butterfly's wings can set off a cascade of events that could not have been predicted or anticipated. And thus, weather is unpredictable. Economics is unpredictable. The direction the universe is going is unpredictable. The direction a particle is going is unpredictable. Any dynamic system is unpredictable. Creation itself is unpredictable, no matter how much we might want it to be otherwise. History is unpredictable. People are unpredictable. Women are unpredictable. Even men are sometimes unpredictable. OK, we'll eat chips, drink beer, watch football, burp, and every now and then go invade some country somewhere for no rational reason, but, really, you can't tell exactly when we are going to get up from football and go invading, though it might be generally related to our favorite team losing. And football is unpredictable.

The good news is that the universe, and anything in it, is not a machine. You and I are not just machines made out of meat.

But if the universe, the creation, reveals the character of its creator, then what does all this say about God?

Well, just for starters, God is unpredictable.

My good friend Trevor's voice is telling me to tell you something, and it's not trivial. Trevor (who doesn't believe in God) points out that even though we humans can never know all of the tiny little variations that may have an impact on a dynamic system, taking it in unpredictable directions, those variations can be known by something or someone with the ability to see and recognize them for what they are and for the potential they represent. I would have called that "God." Trevor preferred to call it something like Laplace's Demon, mostly because the concept of God makes him uncomfortable. Laplace himself didn't even call it a Demon, but neither did he call it God. He and Trevor share some of the same emotions with respect to God, I'm thinking, except that Laplace is dead and Trevor works at a bike shop.

Since this is my book, I'm going to go with God.

God is different from us in yet another way: he is that which can see all the variables that we can't see, and thus he can know what will happen, where we cannot. Not only is he the original observer, able to collapse Singularity into Big Bang, and not only can he choose the outcome of any observation on the micro, quantum level, where we cannot, he also can know what will happen on the macro level, as well.

Remembering that he is outside of time and space, and that at the speed of light, all of time happens in a single instant (and it may be a coincidence that Jesus is the light of the world, but I don't think so), then God clearly is in a position to see everything that has happened and will happen. In fact, that's not quite right, because that implies that he is right here with me now looking at the past and at the future from my perspective in time and space. That's just silly. The future and the past don't exist as such for God—they are the same, time as an instant. There's a saying that on the face of it just sounds like someone clever trying to be clever, but in fact represents reality—"Time exists so that everything doesn't happen all at once. Space exists so that it all doesn't happen to you."

Thus all of the tiny, unknowable variables that have avalanched their way through history are his to know, all of the input, all of the outcomes, the entire flow of history known all at once. If you could go the speed of light, then you could know it all, too, but of course the laws of physics, namely Relativity, prevent you from reaching the speed of light. Interesting, that.

If you could enter a black hole, then at the edge of the event horizon, again you would see and know all of time. But of course, then you would be shredded, or to be precise, spaghettified, and would cease to exist. Again, it's interesting that this is a place where we cannot go. God is God, we are not, and never can be.

A mechanistic universe is predictable, and it is clear that our universe is unpredictable both at the quantum and the macro level, the latter from Chaos Theory. The universe is not a machine and doesn't work like a machine. It works like a dynamic, creative system where you will never know exactly what you will get until you get it, and many times, you may not be able to figure out even how you got it, or to know if your ideas about how you got it are actually accurate.

And yet we consider God to be very much like a machine. That is, he is supposed to do what we ask him to do, and when he doesn't, we just don't understand. He is supposed to be predictable. The Bible makes promises, God makes promises, and there they are, right there in print in any translation you want to use, and yet somehow, we don't get it, or maybe it seems more like God doesn't get it.

This chapter on the Chaotic God may just become a chapter on suffering if we aren't careful. Too late.

Let's be careful not to trivialize this. One might be willing to say that suffering is the defining topic in religion in general. It's not a stretch to say that all religions rotate around and are sometimes defined by the existence of suffering on earth and how to deal with it. In Buddhism, suffering in life is caused by desire, and the solution to suffering is to reduce and eliminate desire. Judaism and Christianity both, as religions with eastern roots, reflect that as well. In Hinduism, suffering is caused by the building up of bad karma by not following one's dharma, that is, in our more familiar terms, sin causes suffering. The difference would be that in Hinduism, one's dharma, or duty, is defined by the status of one's birth, so sin becomes defined by your refusal to know your place in the social order, to put it bluntly, and to live up to the obligations required by your social standing. Obligation also figures in heavily in Japanese religions, especially Shintoism, and it pervades the culture: suffering arrives when you do not live up to your obligations to family, friends, company, school, village, and society in general.

The Bible starts with suffering—the book of Job, the first book in the Bible to be written, is a book about suffering and the questions that man asks of God. Our faith and the faith of the Jews starts with the greatest and most profound of questions—what about suffering? Maybe you should go read Job—it's only 42 chapters long. I'll wait.

Done yet? Really, I've got things to do. Here's a quick summary—Job is doing well for himself, and despite his health, wealth, and prosperity, he has not lost his faith. Abe Lincoln said in 1863, "We have been the recipients of the choicest bounties of heaven. We have been preserved, these many years, in peace and prosperity. We have grown in numbers, wealth, and power, as no other nation has ever grown. But we have forgotten God,"[51] and Hosea wrote something in God's voice that was pretty similar sometime earlier than that: "When I fed them, they were satisfied; when they were satisfied, they became proud; then they forgot me."[52] This was not Job—he was a man of God, a loyal humble servant, a superb role model in faith for others to emulate.

Then the story takes a turn and becomes something that we really just don't know how to handle, if we are paying attention and not overlaying the story with our presuppositions about the character of God. This book, the first book written in the Bible in times lost in antiquity, is among the most subtle and profound books ever written, as great a demonstration that the Bible is not just another religious volume as any other book in all of scripture, and it gives us a picture of God that flies in the face of most of our modern theology and understanding of God, even in the face of what we practice and say in evangelism.

---

[51] Proclamation appointing a National Fast Day, March 30, 1863. The Collected Works of Abraham Lincoln, ed. Roy P. Basler, vol. 6, p. 156

[52] Hosea 13:6 (NIV)

We seem to have created a mechanical, wind-up God that we preach and teach and share with others, and it is not the God of Job. Well, it is, but we've no sense of this God. The God that we preach and teach and share is a God of love. God loves us. God is love. Jesus loves me this I know, for the Bible tells me so. God loves you and has a wonderful plan for your life. The greatest love story ever told. Greater love has no man than to give his life for his brother. This is what we say.

I had some young men at my house the other day for brownie bits and Dr. Pepper. I asked them what God was all about, and they said, God loves us. That's what he's all about.

Then I asked them, what does that mean? When we say that God loves us, what do we mean? How does that play out in our lives?

They fumbled around a bit, didn't really offer substantive answers, so I changed the question to, what doesn't it mean? If God loves us (and he does) and he is a God of love (and he is), then what *doesn't* that imply?

One of them, Josh, one of my favorites, was spot-on. He said it doesn't mean that God gives us everything that we want. It doesn't mean that he protects us from everything that might happen to us.

So, in Job, God and Satan are sitting around drinking Dr. Pepper and watching football, and Satan (who is evil like this) says to God, yo, God, check out Job.

No, that's not what happens. What happens is, God (who is not evil and is a God of love) said to Satan, yo, Satan, check out Job. He's awesome.

Satan says back to God, well, duh, of course. You've protected him from bad things happening to him. Of course he loves you—why wouldn't he? Take all of that good stuff away from him, and he'll be off you like water off a duck's back.

So God says, take your best shot. Just don't kill him.

Right away, I have a problem with this version of God. There's a lot of folks I know and love who tell me the Bible is literally true. I'm thinking they might skip this part in their hearts and minds, because this doesn't sound like a God of love. "Take your best shot"?! What's up with that?

So Satan takes a large number of pretty good shots, strips Job of everything he has—crops, livestock, servants (all by raiding parties, so we could blame this on human sin), children (a mighty wind—no human sin in that one), and then his health, and left him sitting on an ash heap scraping his sores and listening to his nagging wife. And then he says, after she helpfully encourages him to curse God and die, "Shall we accept good from God and not trouble?"

Summing up: Job knows that God is responsible. He doesn't say "God allowed these things to happen." He doesn't say, "God's ways are mysterious."

He doesn't say, "This is a fallen world." He says, "God has given me this to deal with, and that's part of the deal."

I have very close friends named John and Renee who lost a little girl in childbirth, stillborn. They also have a son with severe CP and an adopted girl with fetal alcohol syndrome. After they lost their daughter, more than one person (or so it is in my memory) told them that they must have sinned to have lost a daughter like that.

All of Job's friends did the same thing, one after another. This is the way a mechanical God works. We sin, he punishes, so if it looks like we are being punished, then we must have sinned. (We also think that if we obey, God blesses with wealth, so if we have wealth, we must have been blessed, and if not, then we must be disobedient.) (Baaaaaad theology.)

The Bible takes great pains right in this first book to demonstrate to us that this is not the way God works. God is not a machine. He's not predictable. We may want to have a mechanistic God in a mechanistic universe, because as far as other people are concerned, when they sin, they should be punished. As far as we ourselves are concerned, we are grateful for grace, because then we don't have to get punished as badly as we deserve, sometimes not at all. But we really really want others to be punished. Grace is for me. Not so much for them.

Actually, one of Job's friends did not accuse him of having sinned. Job, by the way, denied having sinned, denied deserving the pain and suffering that God had visited upon him. The book doesn't cut him much slack—it says, "So these three men stopped answering Job, because he was righteous in his own eyes."[53] But the truth was that Job had not lusted after women or committed adultery, had treated his servants well and fairly, was generous to the poor, the widows, the orphans, had not trusted in his wealth, had not gloated over his enemies' misfortunes, had opened his doors to strangers, had helped the blind and the lame, had followed the spirit and the letter of the law. He had loved God and loved his neighbour. He honoured God and his greatness and majesty, ascribing to him the glories of creation and beyond, saying, 'these are but the outer fringe of his works; how faint the whisper we hear of him! Who then can understand the thunder of his power?"[54]

Then the young man Elihu answers in disgust, and his answer is not the kind and loving answer that we would have hoped for: he asks Job and his friends how they can dare to question God at all, ever, on any subject at any time. It doesn't matter if Job is as pure as the driven snow or as evil as Lucifer himself; God will do what God will do, and what God does is never evil and always

---

[53] Job 32:1 (NIV)
[54] Job 26: 14 (NIV)

good. God is good, all the time, and the evil that we want to ascribe to God rebounds upon us.

And then God speaks, and again, it's not what we want to hear: God has no need to justify what he does. He is God. He does what God will do. You don't get to ask those questions and expect an answer.

For this is the message of the entire Bible, and it starts in the first book, the book of Job: God is God, and you are not. There is no story in the Bible that is not this story.

As much as we want to understand God and his ways, as much as we want to apply our vast abilities as reasoning creatures to God and his creation, and as gracious and forgiving as he might be, that's the answer. He's God. You're not. You can be as aggravated as you want for as long as you want, but that's his final answer.

Now, you might feel at this moment like you knew this already. No big deal. Where's the big surprise?

Let's talk some more about suffering, and prayer. Job's real problem was that he was focused on Job's real problem. He had lost everything unfairly, and God wasn't listening or answering his prayers. For Job it was, finally, all about Job. He had an understanding of his relationship with God that God was supposed to prevent these kinds of things from happening. Job's tragedy was immense, but it was Job's tragedy. While the rest of the planet was spinning around blissfully unaware of Job's existence, while the universe continued to expand even more rapidly all the time, while stars were conceived and born and lived and died, while galaxies formed and collided, while black holes slowly evaporated, while races of peoples were slaughtered by other races of people and human history ebbed and flowed, Job's tragedy was his own and it defined God in his entirety for Job and his friends, except for Elihu the younger. The universe of sorrow and suffering that surrounding and overwhelmed Job became the entire universe, and the role of God became to deal with Job's suffering. It became all about God and Job.

And so it has become with our modern, western, individualistic faith. Our mechanistic God has as his job the task of keeping us comfortable and out of pain. We are quick to praise God when the good times roll, but when tragedy strikes, suddenly we have no answers. "God is good" has come to mean "God is good to me," very much like "God has a plan" has come to mean "God has a plan for my life."

God is good. God loves me. God sent his son to die for me. So God must care about me and my life, and since he is good, then he is supposed to be good to me.

So my children will not get sick and die. I will not lose my job or my house or my wife. My friends will not die. God will hear and answer my prayers. If I pray long enough and hard enough, if I pray and fast, if I combine my praying and fasting with others who pray and fast, if we gang up on God, then he will hear our prayers and it'll happen. God is a machine. Push all the right buttons, and you get what the machine is designed to give you.

And when I push all the right praying and fasting buttons, and people die anyway, people who die too young, too soon, too full of promise and potential, when new babies are stillborn and toddlers drown, when fathers of children die and leave mothers alone with their kids, when teens are taken, then I have no answers, for God is good and is supposed to protect me.

Here's the answer you want: God cares, he loves you, he travels with you through the pain and hurt, he will take you to safe places and make you more than you were. He restored Job's wealth and gave him new children, servants, herds and friends.

Here's the answer you don't want: it's not your story. It's God's. You will suffer because suffering is what we do as humans. It is a product of love and choice and free will. It's part of relationships and caring. Love less, hurt less. Love more, hurt more. Love as God loves, and you can't imagine the hurt. But it's not your story. It's his.

David sinned with Bathsheba. You know it. He committed adultery, got her pregnant, had her husband killed, covered it up, abused his power, took advantage of his position, put himself above the law into an exalted place. You know the story. He got caught, confessed his sin, was forgiven. Case closed.

Except for the baby. It was dying. The baby didn't do anything wrong. It was the most innocent person in the whole story. But God was taking this baby away.

David fasted, prayed, agonized, prostrated himself, humbled himself, cried out to God. He did everything anyone of us has ever done to change the mind of God, to intervene, to save the life of this innocent child.

And then:

> On the seventh day the child died. David's servants were afraid to tell him that the child was dead, for they thought, "While the child was still living, we spoke to David but he would not listen to us. How can we tell him the child is dead? He may do something desperate." David noticed that his servants were whispering among themselves and he realized the child was dead. "Is the child dead?" he asked. "Yes," they replied, "he is dead." Then David got up from the ground. After he had washed, put on lotions and changed his clothes, he went into the house

of the Lord and worshiped. Then he went to his own house, and at his request they served him food, and he ate. His servants asked him, "Why are you acting this way? While the child was alive, you fasted and wept, but now that the child is dead, you get up and eat!" He answered, "While the child was still alive, I fasted and wept. I thought, 'Who knows? The Lord may be gracious to me and let the child live.' But now that he is dead, why should I fast? Can I bring him back again? I will go to him, but he will not return to me."[55]

David understood well that God is not a machine: he is not predictable. He might have healed the child. He did not. It was over. There's no room for anger at God in this story. It was finished. God is God. He will do what he will do. It's his story.

And the question is not, why doesn't God love us more? The question is, why does he love us at all? It is not, why doesn't he heal us, protect us, shelter us from evil? It is, why does he do anything at all for us?

He is not a machine. Machines do not love. But he is not a machine. He does what he will do. And do you really want to know the mind of God? It is not yours to know.

---

[55] 2 Samuel 12: 18-22 (NIV)

Chapter 9
Holy, Holy, Wholly Complex God

There is more to learn about the Chaotic God, but it will come in the context of the Complex God. The Chaotic God is the God of the Butterfly Effect—a tiny little touch on a dynamic system can cause huge, unpredictable changes in that system, and when the system is you or the church or the nations or all of humanity, then those tiny little imperceptible touches can change the flow of history. All it takes is seeing all of time, knowing all the variables and all the possible paths that a touch can influence.

We of course cannot see all of time, may not in fact be able to see anything meaningful of time at all, since the moment we occupy of time is unimaginably small and transient, the past we used to occupy no longer exists, and the future is not here yet and does not exist for us. But for God, of course, all of time exists in a single moment.

We cannot know all the variables—they are too tiny, too insignificant for us to notice, though they hold the potential to change all of history. And for us, the only path that exists is the one that appears after we have made our observation so that the reality of that path becomes realized, *realized*, as it were.

We are not God. God was not in the "great and powerful wind" that "tore the mountains apart and shattered the rocks" in front of Elijah, and "was not in the earthquake" and "was not in the fire." But "after the fire came a gentle whisper"[56]; that God of the gentle whisper can touch the tiny touch and do great and mighty things, and we may not even be able to find proof or even evidence of his touch afterwards. Was it a miracle? Was it natural? It is all natural. It is all a miracle.

What science has long wanted and pretended to do is to reduce nature to that which can be understood, and it does this by breaking things down into smaller and smaller parts and interacting forces. The Quantum has shown us that at the smallest level, not only do we not understand things better, we don't understand things at all. But somehow we can still pretend that nothing is anything more than the sum of its parts. We play foolish mathematical games that can intimidate those who are not as fluent. We share, for example, 98.5 percent of our DNA with chimpanzees, so it must be that we and they are pretty much the same. We share more than 99 percent of our DNA with each other, and so every human must be pretty much the same as every other human. There's no difference worth talking about. And of course, the universe is pretty much

---

[56] 1 Kings 19:11b-12 (NIV)

empty, as we examined earlier. Since there's nothing really here, there's nothing really here.

But it is the places where matter exists, as tiny as it is, that define the universe itself, and it is the tiny little differences that make all the difference.

For example, from Reuters: *Tiny genetic changes add up to huge differences* (emphasis mine) when human DNA is compared to that of chimpanzees, researchers said in a report that explains how people and apes can be so close, yet so far apart.

> Clearly, the genomic differences between humans and chimps are much more complicated than conventional wisdom has portrayed," Asao Fujiyama and colleagues wrote in their report, published in the journal Nature. While the genes and other DNA may look the same in chimpanzees and humans, the proteins they eventually code for can be very different. This supports what genetic researchers have been saying lately—that subtle changes in the genetic code that reach far beyond the genes themselves may be extremely important to biology."[57]

It is patently obvious to the most casual of observers that each human is different from every other human in critical and defining ways, though we are 99 percent the same. Similarities? Clearly. We are bound together in community by our similarities, but defined as individuals by our differences, each person as amazingly unique as we are also stunningly similar. Reductionism, in trying legitimately to find out what makes us similar so that we can be described as a species and dealt with medically, psychologically and sociologically, loses our individuality in the process because it ignores the influence of tiny variables that can hardly be measured.

Again, this time from *Science Daily*: "A study led by McGill University researchers has demonstrated that small differences between individuals at the DNA level can lead to dramatic differences in the way genes produce proteins. These, in turn, are responsible for the vast array of differences in physical characteristics between individuals."[58]

And again,

---

[57] May 26, 2004 Yahoo! Science News
[58] *ScienceDaily*, Jan. 20, 2008

In a blow to human vanity, researchers now say that people have about the same number of genes as a small flowering plant or a tiny worm. The new estimate is down sharply from just three years ago. "We (humans) don't look very impressive in the competition," said Dr. Francis Collins, co-author of the new analysis by the international group that decoded the human genome. The new estimate is 20,000 to 25,000 genes, a drop from the 30,000 to 40,000 the same group of scientists published in 2001. "But the complexity of the human body arises from more than just its genetic parts list," experts said. "It's not just the number of genes that matters," said Eric Lander of the Broad Institute. "It really is how nature uses these genes."

"In comparison to simpler organisms," Collins said, "Humans benefit more from genes that turn out multiple proteins rather than one, and from complex proteins that do more than one job. And anyway, lots of biological complexity is based not on individual proteins but on combinations, which can create lots of variety from the proteins found in people."[59]

And from Mark Houser at Harvard, "Charles Darwin argued in his 1871 book The Descent of Man that the difference between human and nonhuman minds is 'one of degree and not of kind.' Scholars have long upheld that view, pointing in recent years to genetic evidence showing that we share some 98 percent of our genes with chimpanzees. But if our shared genetic heritage can explain the evolutionary origin of the human mind, then why isn't a chimpanzee writing this essay, or singing backup for the Rolling Stones or making a soufflé? Indeed, mounting evidence indicates that, in contrast to Darwin's theory of a continuity of mind between humans and other species, a profound gap separates our intellect from the animal kind."[60]

The key challenge to Reductionism in science today is found in Complexity Theory, and the key to Complexity is what is called *emergence*. Emergence is the spontaneous self-organization that occurs unpredictably and uncontrollably when dynamic systems reach a tipping point, a place where either the numbers of organisms involved in the system reaches a certain, ill-defined number, or when enough tiny variables (that Butterfly Effect again) combine to launch the system into a new direction. Tiny differences in the way that proteins code result in huge differences between species, between humans and chimps, in our example above, or in combinations of proteins that spontaneously work

---

[59] CBS News, 3 Aug 2008, www.cbsnews.com/stories/2004/10/20/tech/main650405.shtml

[60] Marc Hauser in <u>Scientific American</u>; Sep 2009, Vol. 301 Issue 3, p44-51

together to take simpler things and turn them into vastly more complicated things.

It is not just the number of genes that matters, as Lander says above, but the way those genes work together. The way that nature uses those genes emerges from the combination, from the relationships that emerge between the genes themselves. Complexity is all about simple things producing complicated results, and the results can't be predicted and are not foreordained in the individuals that make up the system. It is the interactions that define the system, not the isolated individuals. Once again, it's the rules, the laws of nature that determine the emergence of complex systems, the interactions relationally between the members of the system.

There are numbers of examples in *Life, the Universe, and Everything*, but let's throw a few more in to aid in understanding a counterintuitive claim for emergent complexity.

For example, when do locusts swarm?

> Scientists have finally figured out the exact moment when a jumbled swarm of creatures becomes an organized, unified, and sometimes terrifying, mass. Examining a group of desert locusts, researchers found that at low densities, the insects were unorganized and went their separate ways. But when the group's density increased, the bugs fell into an orderly line and began to follow the same direction. When there were a few of them together, they did not coalesce. As the group grew to 10 to 25 members, the locusts got closer to each other, but still did not move in unison. It was only when the researchers placed about 30 locusts in the arena that the insects fell into a line and started moving in the same direction. The march of the locusts is a bit of a mystery since they have no leader and each one can only communicate with close neighbors.[61]

There is a critical and, as we said above, ill-defined number of locusts that determines the difference between milling about randomly and emergent organization. The number is not as ill-defined here as it might be—it's "about 30," which is more precise than many examples we will find in nature, but it illustrates the point beautifully. A few locusts don't swarm. It takes a certain number for the self-organization to emerge, and even after it happens, we're not really sure why it happens nor how everything progresses from that point onward.

---

[61] *Why Locusts Swarm: New Study Finds 'Tipping Point'*, Sara Goudarzi, LiveScience, 1 June 2006

It happens at the bacterial level, as well:

> There is a perception that single-celled organisms are asocial, but that is misguided," said Andre Levchenko, assistant professor of biomedical engineering in The Johns Hopkins University's Whiting School of Engineering and an affiliate of the university's Institute for NanoBioTechnology. "When bacteria are under stress, which is the story of their lives, they team up and form this collective called a biofilm. If you look at naturally occurring biofilms, they have very complicated architecture. They are like cities with channels for nutrients to go in and waste to go out.[62]

Dr. Steve Diggle adds,

> We can no longer consider bacteria to be single celled entities living and dividing in isolation of each other. They can communicate with each other, preferentially direct aid toward close relatives and even cheat on each other. Bacterial populations are a lot more sophisticated than many people have thought.[63]

And again from Princeton researchers,

> Microbes may be smarter than we think. A new study by Princeton University researchers shows for the first time that bacteria don't just react to changes in their surroundings—they anticipate and prepare for them. The findings, reported in Science, challenge the prevailing notion that only organisms with complex nervous systems have this ability.
>
> "What we have found is the first evidence that bacteria can use sensed cues from their environment to infer future events," says Saeed Tavazoie, an associate professor in the department of Molecular Biology. "The two lines of investigation came together nicely to show how simple biochemical networks can perform sophisticated computational tasks."[64]

We should probably leave it at that, since the point has been made that bacteria self-organize, but it's hard to resist taking it to the next threat level:

---

[62] *Together We Stand: Bacteria Organize Into Biofilms To Survive Hostile Zones*, ScienceDaily, Nov. 14, 2007
[63] *Bacteria Can Cheat On Their Mates*, ScienceDaily, Dec. 3, 2007, Dr Steve Diggle, University of Nottingham
[64] *Thinking Ahead: Bacteria Anticipate Coming Changes In Their Environment*, ScienceDaily, June 19, 2008

> Bacteria that know how to disable or block the efficacy of multiple drugs are highly educated organisms…they have downloaded genetic cheat codes from other resistant bacteria into their own DNA. Multidrug-resistant staph, for example, hijacked genes from a bug called *enterococcus* that have made it resistant to vancomycin—the drug of last resort…One strain of of multidrug-resistant *acinetobacter baumannii* carries the largest collection of genetic upgrades ever discovered in a single organism. Out of its 52 genes dedicated to defeating antibiotics, radiation, and other weapons of mass bacterial destruction, nearly all have been bootlegged from other bad bugs.[65]

One might note that bacteria change with intent and specificity, not just to respond to threats in their environment, but to predict what threats those might be and how to get around them by *downloading cheat codes from other resistant bacteria*, not by mutating randomly and being selected for survival. Bacteria self-organize outside what we understand to be the standard model of evolutionary theory in order to ensure that they survive and thrive.

What this means for science ought to be paradigm-shattering, though it has not yet reached that point, almost solely because most research is still being done from a reductionist perspective. As clear as it is that taking things apart is a great way to begin to understand them, it seems to be true that in order truly to understand them, we have to understand how all the parts interact. A brief snippet on water will illustrate what we mean:

> Water makes up 70 percent of the Earth's surface and is the main component—about 80 percent—of all living things. But it is far from ordinary. The solid form of water—ice—floats instead of sinking, as with most substances. Water stores heat very well. And its high surface tension shows how its molecules hate coming apart. Understanding the peculiarities of water requires detailed study of its molecular interactions. "We think we understand everything there is about a single water molecule," Saykally said. "What we don't understand so well is how they interact with each other."[66]

That bears repeating—"We think we understand everything there is about a single water molecule. What we don't understand so well is how they interact with each other." Which is to say that if we don't understand how water molecules interact, we may not understand anything at all about water.

---

[65] *The Invisible Enemy*, Wired Magazine, Steve Silberman, Feb 2007
[66] LiveScience.com, *The New Mystery of Water*, By Michael Schirber, 01 December, 2004

And when the interactions are quantum, all bets are off:

> All the bonds affecting water molecules are ultimately caused by quantum effects, but hydrogen bonds are the result of one of the strangest quantum phenomena: so-called zero-point vibrations. These constant vibrations are a product of the impossibility of pinning down the total energy of a system with absolute precision.
>
> Even if the universe itself froze over and its temperature plunged to absolute zero, zero-point vibrations would still be going strong, propelled by energy from empty space.
>
> Just take some water and swap the hydrogen for atoms of its heavier isotope deuterium. You end up with a liquid that is chemically identical, yet poisonous to all but the most primitive organisms. "The only difference is in the zero-point energy."
>
> Researchers are now investigating this deep link between quantum effects and life. The results are often unexpected, and challenge simplistic assumptions about how life works.
>
> Certainly the fashionable view that the secret of life can be summed up in a catalogue of genes and the proteins they code for looks simplistic.
>
> It is becoming clear that they cannot carry out even their most basic functions without direct help from molecules of the colourless, odourless curiosity that comes out of the tap.
>
> "Without water, it is all just chemistry, but add water and you get biology.
>
> "It's the magic ingredient that turns lifeless powders on laboratory shelves into living things."[67]

If we don't understand how water molecules interact, we may not understand anything at all about water. True for water, true for bacteria and parasites, true for locusts. True for all of the biosphere? For humans? True for all of nature? True for the universe itself?

The answer seems to be yes. It is the interactions in nature that define nature, that define life, the universe, and everything. Reductionism can take us only so far, and from that point on, it is Complexity that needs to define scientific

---

[67] *Water: The quantum elixir*, Robert Matthews, 8 April 2006, NewScientist.com news service

inquiry. Reductionist science tells us that we need to examine things in isolation from other things, to reduce the outside noise and influence, the uncontrollable variables that can untrack and mangle results of an experiment or investigation.

But Complexity tells us that everything is interrelated, that nothing exists and functions in a real way in isolation. Everything is related to everything else. Everything is vastly more than just the sum of its parts, even something as apparently simple as a water molecule or a bacterium, and the emergent relationships between things are unpredictable, complex, elegant, and fundamental.

For no apparent reason other than the laws of physics compel it to happen, quarks and electrons of no size, mass, or existence as we understand it spin into existence out of energy. For no real reason other than particle interactions, quarks form protons and neutrons, and eventually combine with electrons to form simple atoms. For no obvious reason other than the compulsion of gravity, simple atoms draw together into immense gas clouds and create burning stars, and the rest of the elements emerge in time to create the dust of life and the core of planets. For no reason at all, life emerges from non-life, complexity emerges from simplicity, intelligence emerges from collections of neurons and synapses which have emerged from, I don't know, ultimately just particle interactions, and the vast incredible brilliance of a universe that exists for no apparent reason gives rise to creatures which interact with the universe to give that universe a real existence.

It is only the interaction that we have with the universe that cause reality itself to be possible, and yet that reality is not what it seems to be, nor was it ever, nor will it ever be what it seems to be. Reality itself is dependent on interactions both in a linear, historical sort of way and in a quantum, backwards-in-time sort of way with no linearity whatsoever.

Now, again, what does any of this have to do with God?

Chapter 10

The Gentle Whisper of Math

As far as science is concerned, some think that this leads to the Anthropic Principle, which simply enough states that the parameters of the existence of life alone, not to mention those of the existence of human life, are so tight and unlikely that it seems most logical to assume that the universe was designed or created to produce humans. (Since we wrote at length about this in the other book, we'll let you go read that one, along with some of the comments we recorded in chapter 5 in this book.) On the basis of the science itself, this is a reasonable conclusion to reach, if controversial and not universally shared. It takes no leap of faith or even of logic to get here. And it is only after we arrive at this point that many are pretty sure that they don't like here and they want to go back.

And so they do, back into a reductionist worldview, which hides much of what they seek, because they don't want to know what they need to know, and do know already, in order to peel back the hidden, quantum layers of a now-terrifying universe. Oddly enough, reductionism is more comforting, though it leads to meaninglessness and purposelessness, because they can pretend to hold onto a strict rationalism, the mind once again supreme and in control of knowledge.

Thus many scientists feel exalted and uplifted because they have figured things out in such a way as to eliminate the presumed importance of humanity and any meaning or purpose in life. Some seem positively to glory in the meaninglessness of life, as though it is a release from something onerous and nasty, and that because their minds have taken them to this point. As long as logic and reason (and logical and reasonable laws of nature) are driving the bus, they don't seem to care that the ride really doesn't go anywhere.

For people of faith, there are some things about God that need to be explored. We suffer from a similar malaise—we want to hold onto our understanding of God and his universe. In so doing, we reduce God to something that he isn't, but that we want him to be. We are practicing our own version of reductionism—reducing God to the God we can comprehend.

Just to make us all feel extra bad, let's do a comparison between us and scientists who do the same.

Scientists: everything is an accident. Us: nothing is an accident.

Scientists: there are no miracles. Us: everything is a miracle.

Scientists: nothing is designed. Us: everything is designed.

Scientists: nothing is planned. Us: everything is planned.

Scientists: nothing was coordinated. Us: everything was coordinated.

Scientists: everything took a long time to happen. Us: everything was done instantly.

Scientists: Big Bang, a tiny fraction of a second, 13.7 billion years ago. Us: six days, 6,000 years ago.

Scientists: Evolution, random mutation, natural selection, randomness rules. Us: Adam, dust, Eve, rib, a purpose for everything, everything for a purpose.

Scientists: the universe is indifferent to our existence. Us: God loves me and has a wonderful plan for my life.

No wonder we don't get along. So let's talk about Us.

We have somehow become people who insist on absolutely literal readings of some parts of scripture, the point of which we may be missing, and at the same time, we are people for whom other parts of scripture need to be reinterpreted according to, I don't know, culture, history, politics, semantics, whatever, and there again, we may be missing the point.

It must be said that this is true for everyone; right, left, center, liberal, conservative, heretic, fanatic, priest, prophet, pastor, teacher, theologians, Jesus Seminarians, illiterates (the only group I won't manage to offend here), everyone. We all pick and choose what parts we will believe and what parts we will ignore or minimize the importance of, and most of us are terrified that we might discover that the world is round. In so doing, we reduce God to being smaller and less significant than he is.

Let's list the ways we have reduced him:

He has become far more the God of the supernatural than the natural. Science to us has become an offense to God, any attempt to explain what exists by the laws of nature, a heresy. Somehow the laws of nature seem to us to have been a big surprise to God, as though he made the universe and suddenly said to himself, Hey, where did those come from? Dang! I hate it when that happens!

Thus he reveals himself primarily through miracles rather than through, well, nonmiracles, and miracles are things that happen in violation of the laws of nature.

Except for those of us for whom he has become far more the God of the natural than the supernatural. We have a fear that we won't look smart to our smart, reductionist friends, so we have thrown away the miraculous God altogether.

Thus he reveals himself primarily through, well, nonmiracles rather than through miracles, and miracles are things that happen in violation of the laws of nature. So they don't happen. The science of the moment (which is really the science of Newton and Leibniz rather than Einstein and Bohr) doesn't allow for miracles. We're really just not going to talk about Big Bang or Quantum Mechanics if it's all right with you. (Butterflies? What butterflies?)

Rather than being revealed through scripture, God has been taken captive by it, or at least by the interpretations we impose upon it, which in turn derive from our own desires about the way we think it should be and the things that we think it should say, each of us sometimes too concerned about some things and too little concerned about others.

Normally what we would do here is to enter into a big argument, me trying to prove my points and you getting hostile enough to want to exercise your second amendment rights. That's the nature of debate about God and science these days—hostility and unwillingness to think, and lest you think that I'm accusing one side or the other of being the guiltier non-thinking party, well, think again.

So we're not going to do that, that is, get into the back and forthing. Instead, we're just going to look back at the science and see what it might say about God and his character.

A brief history of the universe seems to be in order, with some review. As much as the scientists (and, it seems, the Protestant evangelicals) did not want to admit it, the universe bounced into being in a tiny tiny fraction of a second out of nothing just shy of 14 billion years ago. There was no "before" that moment, there was nowhere for that event to take place, because time and space did not exist at the moment; more precisely, space-time did not yet exist.

And then, suddenly, they did, and along with space-time arrived the laws of physics written in the language of the universe, mathematics. Why? God alone knows. He seems to be a mathematician and a physicist. Eugene Wigner, Nobel Prize winner in physics said that "the enormous usefulness of mathematics in the natural sciences is something bordering on the mysterious and . . . there is no rational explanation for it." And Richard Feynman, also a Nobel Prize winner in physics, wrote, "Why nature is mathematical is a mystery. . . . The fact that there are rules at all is a kind of miracle." The universe started out with what we might call a natural miracle, the miracle of nature, but really without any nature to speak of yet—just a language, and the language held the laws of physics. There was no law of nature to produce the universe, just to be clear, since nature didn't exist yet.

But the laws of physics were not like traffic laws, because traffic laws are macro laws for the macro world, except where I desperately hope that God has quantumly predestined that I do not get the speeding ticket that I really just deserve to get, hoping beyond hope that the cop does not quantumly observe my ticket into reality. The laws of physics applied first to the micro world, the quantum, where things are not reasonable and rational in the way that we perceive them to be.

And there seemed to be a joyful compulsion to the laws of physics, a compelling of space-time to begin to do things. Before the first second of creation was finished, particles spun themselves into existence out of energy and were immediately compelled to begin getting organized into structure. Forces needed particles, and particles needed forces, a delicate *pas de deux* that gave the universe the high energy choreography, a simple *entrenous* that led inexorably and inevitably to protons and neutrons and nuclei, to atoms of hydrogen and helium, to gas clouds that were trillions of miles long and heated up to millions of degrees, to star birth and somehow, miraculously, naturally, to thermonuclear combustion and physical chemistry, the creation from simple atoms of much more complex atoms.

There was the burning star miracle that took the universe from beryllium to carbon, a resonance that was predicted by atheist Fred Hoyle to exist because in order for us to be here, an impossible resonance had to exist, and so it did:

> Would you not say to yourself, "some super-calculating intellect must have designed the properties of the carbon atom, otherwise the chance of my finding such an atom through the blind forces of nature would be utterly miniscule." Of course, you would! A common sense interpretation of the facts suggests that a super-intellect has monkeyed with physics, as well as with chemistry and biology, and that there are no blind forces worth speaking about in nature. The numbers one calculates from the facts seem to me so overwhelming as to put this conclusion almost beyond question. The probability of life originating at random is so utterly miniscule as to make the random concept absurd.[68]

And hence to nitrogen, oxygen, sodium, magnesium, silicon, phosphorous and the rest of the elements needed for life and for life-producing and –supporting planets, planets that need an iron core, intense heat and pressures caused by gravitational forces, plate tectonics, the right temperature range for life, water, air, energy and the ability to convert energy into food, and food into

---

[68] Fred Hoyle, "The Universe: Past and Present Reflections." *Engineering and Science*, November, 1981. p 8-12

energy. But all of the elements were trapped inside stars which needed to die and explode inside galaxies of many stars that could capture and contain the elements and form planets from the detritus of dead stars.

There are at each juncture vast leaps of organization that need to take place between one stage and the next, leaps that cannot take place incrementally or gradually. In *The Emergence of Everything*, Harold Morowitz lists them in chronological order:[69]

1. Something rather than nothing	2. Nonuniform universe	3. Stars
4. Periodic Table	5. Planets	6. Geospheres
7. Metabolism	8. Cells	9. Cells with organelles
10. Multicellularity	11. The Neuron	12. Animal-ness
13. Chordate-ness	14. Vertebrates	15. Fish to amphibians
16. Reptiles	17. Mammals	18. Arboreal Mammals
19. Primates	20. Great Apes	21. Hominization
22. Tool making	23. Language	24. Agriculture
25. Technology and Urbanization	26. Philosophy	27. The Spirit

We have talked about many of them, asking the questions and looking at the process: Why is there something rather than nothing in our universe? How do you go from nothing to something, and when the something is full of nothing, how does that nothing become something? Now that we have a universe, why was it almost perfect thermodynamically, and why did those tiny variations in temperature and density result in the potential for order in the universe?

An important step that Morowitz missed is the matter/anti-matter problem: Where did the anti-matter go, and why is there matter in the universe? Then stars, elements, planets, and those first steps that started with math and proceeded through cosmology, physics, physical chemistry, and chemistry to bio-chemistry and biology, each step a leap, a vault over a yawning precipice of complexity.

And of course, in what might be the most yawning chasm of them all, how do you go from non-life to life, from inanimate to animate, from star dust, the dregs of dead stars, to something that is alive? The odds of life appearing by random chance or accident anywhere in the universe seem so small as to verge on the literally impossible, just barely allowing for life on our planet in this nondescript, bland part of a dullish galaxy, and then only because a large number of unlikely events lined up like butterflies to nudge life into being.

---

[69] *The Emergence of Everything: How the World Became Complex*, Harold Morowitz, pub Oxford University Press 2002, pp vii-viii

We're not going to try to deal with life ultimately producing radio talk-show hosts, which seems to me like heading in the opposite direction complexity-wise.

But the universe needs life, and the process of progress in the universe seemed to aim directly at enabling life to emerge, and from life, intelligent life, the sentient life forms that the universe needed to enable its own existence.

We are faced then with a fascinating set of circumstances: life is so unlikely that its existence is, according to Francis Crick, "almost a miracle," at least on this planet, with the odds against life forming by random chance, according to Roger Penrose, 10 to the 10 to the 123rd to one, against, an unfathomably large number that would take a piece of paper the square of the square of the size of our universe just to write down. But the need for intelligent life in this universe is absolute—it has to be here in order for reality itself to exist.

So. Did the butterfly flap its wings to set off that unlikely avalanche of interconnected events that ultimately resulted in the arrival of humankind on the shores of the cosmos? Did the ordering power of Complexity drive a new universe that was overwhelming in its lack of entropy toward that creature that, when it opened its eyes and caressed the universe with thought, caused it all to come into being?

Do we have a universe without an initial observation? Do we have an ordered universe without an orderer? Do we have a universe with rules, with laws of physics, without a rule-giver? Do we have a universe that is compelled to disorder itself from almost perfect order into an entropic future that includes highly ordered, observing brains without a compulsion, without a compeller? Do we have a universe that is the right size and the right age with the right combination of particles and interactions without someone to lay out the boundaries and, in taking order into chaos, takes chaos into complexity, and complexity into relationship? Do we have a universe that takes relationship into E! and People Magazine? OK, maybe not.

For what we have is a universe that is bound up in itself in intimate, profound, chaotic, complex, quantum interactions, relationships, particle to particle, Jennifer to Brad, Brad to Angelina (Chaos strikes again – I've no idea how that got in here), particle to force, time to space and space to time, gravity to matter and matter to gravity, energy to matter and matter to energy, star-birth to star-death, the stuff of life from the death of stuff, non-life to life, life to the universe, and the universe to life. It is the interactions that define life, the universe and everything, and it is finally relationship writ large that defines God and his creation. Not counting Brad and Jennifer and Angelina.

He is not in the wind or the earthquake or the fire, but he is in the gentle whisper that reaches across to us, from outside of time and space into time and space to seek out that part of his character that the universe reveals—he is a relational God who seeks relationship with his creation, and in that part of his creation which is most like him, the observers, the mind, the consciousness, the wielders of free will, the creatures who can choose this way or that, this belief or that, this relationship or that.

How then can we relate to this God, we who are so tiny and insignificant?

It is time for the fractal Jesus.

Chapter 11

Fractalated Universe

"We ascribe beauty to that which is simple."[70]

"When I am working on a problem I never think about beauty. I only think about how to solve the problem. But when I have finished, if the solution is not beautiful, I know it is wrong."[71]

"It is more important to have beauty in one's equations than to have them fit experiment."[72]

Ignoring experimental accuracy, Einstein took acceleration and gravity to be exactly equal, a breathtaking leap which led him to realize that they were relative to each other. This was to be the basis for his general theory of relativity, a theory scientists often describe as the most beautiful theory ever proposed.[73]

"What separates ordinary theoretical physicists from great ones is their ability to discover physical principles and the symmetries lying behind them. Physicists think a theory is beautiful if it can explain the largest amount of physical data with the simplest mathematical structures. Why does nature use symmetry to express its deepest secrets? No one knows. This is one of the greatest mysteries of all time. I suspect that this is because we are slowly reconstructing the original symmetries that existed at the instant of the big bang, uncovering bits and pieces of new symmetries along the way. If this picture is correct, all the beauty and symmetry we see around us, including sea shells, ice crystals, galaxies, molecules, even sub-atomic particles, are nothing but the pieces of the original symmetry that broke at the instant of the big bang. Nature, at

---

[70] Ralph Waldo Emerson
[71] Buckminster Fuller
[72] Paul Dirac
[73] NewScientist Magazine, Feb 4 2006

its most fundamental level, expresses itself in the most beautiful, elegant and symmetrical way."[74]

In an email interchange with some folks in one of my Google groups, I wrote the following relative to the value of jewelry as a gift from man to woman:

> On the grander subject, to reduce the world to utilitarianism is to say that the only things that have value are the things that are useful, and this ignores the role that beauty plays in the grand scheme of things. Beauty is useful (it attracts men or women, for example, to women or men), but it has a transcendent value that extends far beyond its usefulness. Physics looks for the beautiful, elegant solution, and it is often the simplest solution, so beauty takes us down a path that nature wants us to follow. God himself is not just about how useful things are—why would he have bothered to make a universe with no apparent use, or cause that universe to produce humans, most of whom enjoy a brief moment of either beauty or usefulness, but not really and not for long. There is the beauty of the relationship, the delicate dance of romance and the Texas two-step of deep and abiding friendship. Useful, yes, but with a beauty that has its own value and worth, an elegance that just makes the universe a nicer place to be.

From the elegant simplicity of the Singularity, a cosmos. From an almost nonexistent (in either time or space) interplay between particles and forces, matter. From the simplicity of elementary atoms and gravity, stars and elements. From the simplicity of dust and emergence, life, and from the simplicity of observation, again, a cosmos. From the simplest of things, the most complex of results. That's Complexity Theory, and perhaps that is the way it all happens.

There's something in Chaos that aims us at Complexity, since they are intimately related. Chaos is generally about things falling apart, and Complexity is generally about things coming together. Complexity is called "the edge of Chaos" because it is at that energetic edge between stasis and disaster that new and complex order finds a tiny little gap to squeeze through. That "something" starts with fractals.

Most simple equations that you might have learned in, and may not remember from your math classes, the ones that your teacher asked you to

---

[74] Michio Kaku

graph on homework and tests, had pretty simple solutions, though they may not have seemed simple to you at the time. They would have looked like points, lines, planes, parabolae, circles, ellipses, hyperbolae, and other variations on the themes that would have included the same basic shapes but moved to a different location on the graph.

Nowadays, students can get their calculators or iPhones or Wiis or whatever to graph them and send them to the printer at the front of the classroom, and those of us who are older hate you all with an abiding passion, because we wasted hundreds of hours drawing graphs that might otherwise have been spent watching *The Monkees*. Not that we actually ever missed watching *The Monkees*. What are you thinking?

In Chaos, though, we have a very simple equation that gives us graphs that are the most complicated things man has ever discovered. The equation looks like this:

$$Y = Z^2 + C$$

It's pretty simple, apart from z being a complex number, but c is just a constant. We'll pick random values for z and c, get a new value for y, substitute it in for z, keep doing that over and over, and see what we get. Sometimes we get nothing. But when we get something, we get something called a "fractal" that looks like these from Fractal Recursions, used by permission from Jock Cooper, found along with many other extraordinary images at www.Fractal-recursions.com :

Those don't look like circles or parabolae. On the face of it, they just look ornate and interesting.

But the depths of ornateness and interest have yet to reveal themselves. If we could take you on a little animated journey, you would see that we could in effect dive into these fractals and never come out. What we are really doing is magnifying them, picking any spot. You really need to get on the Internet and see what you can find on YouTube for fractal animations, especially those that zoom in. Jock Cooper's site above has some great zooms.

Since we can't do those here, I'll insert some pictures of a fractal being magnified from *Fractal Cosmos*, published by Amber Lotus (San Francisco). What you will see is beauty, what we call "self-similarity" which is exactly what it sounds like, and ultimately a little bit of infinity, but infinity downwards and inwards. Pay special attention to the magnification under each fractal:

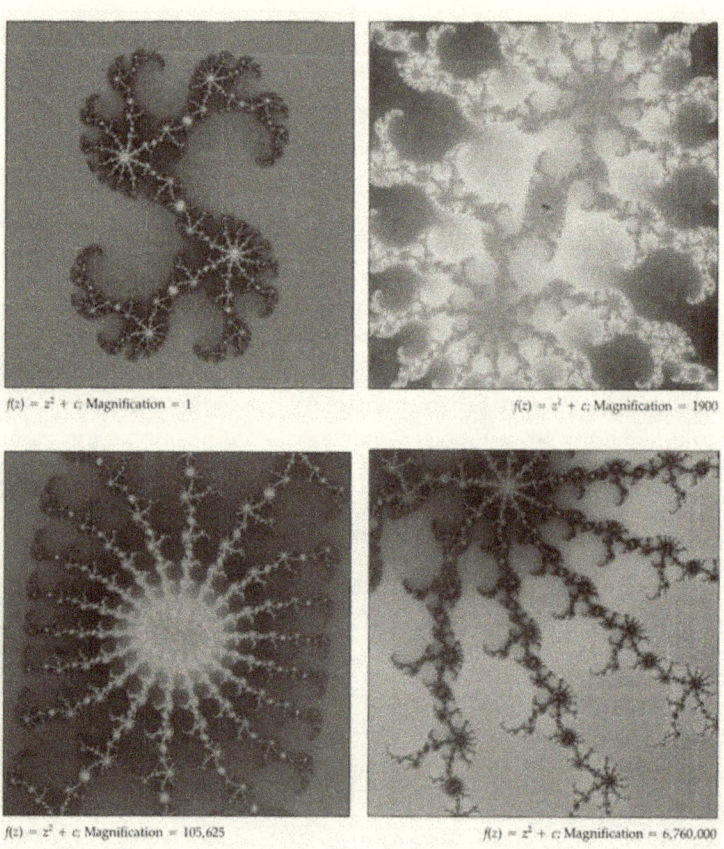

$f(z) = z^2 + c$; Magnification = 1

$f(z) = z^2 + c$; Magnification = 1900

$f(z) = z^2 + c$; Magnification = 105,625

$f(z) = z^2 + c$; Magnification = 6,760,000

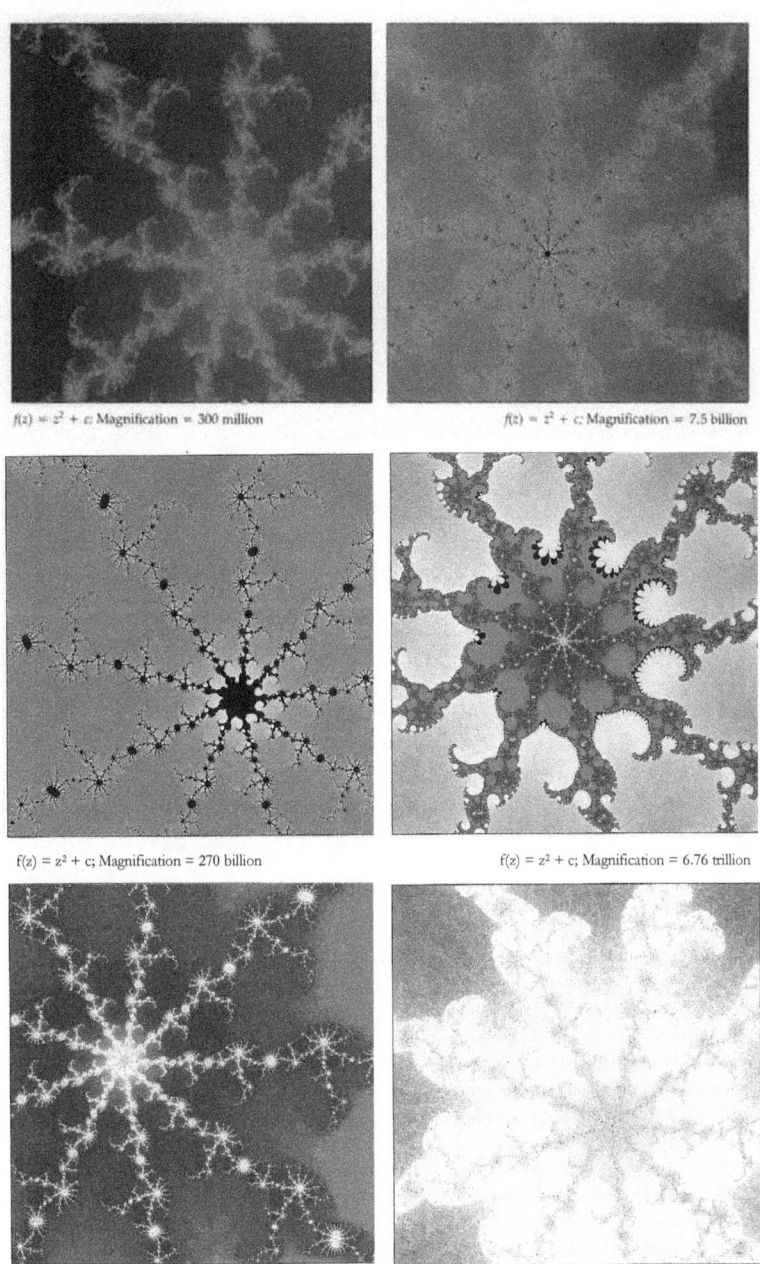

f(z) = z² + c; Magnification = 300 million

f(z) = z² + c; Magnification = 7.5 billion

f(z) = z² + c; Magnification = 270 billion

f(z) = z² + c; Magnification = 6.76 trillion

f(z) = z² + c; Magnification = 169 trillion

f(z) = z² + c; Magnification = 16.9 quadrillion

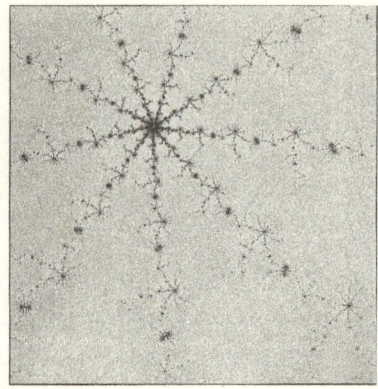 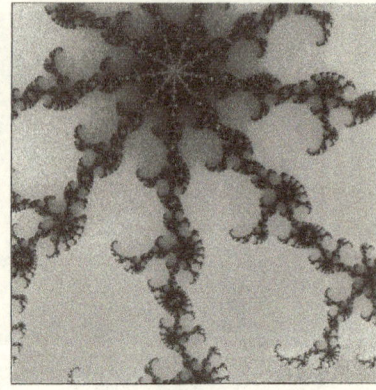

$f(z) = z^2 + c$; Magnification = 1.69 quintillion $f(z) = z^2 + c$; Magnification = 169 quintillion

What you'll notice is a number of things that are going on. No matter how much we zoom, there is self-similarity, but in a creative, unpredictable sort of way. There is variety, diversity, beauty and elegance, so that even though things may initially look all the same, at the same time they look different, and as they look initially look different, they all look the same. The zoom continues forever, which is not to say that we can zoom in on smaller and smaller scales, since sooner or later we will run into the quantum landscape, but rather that we can magnify the image forever. There is infinity hiding within the first image. Every fractal is exactly the same in that regard—self-similarity, stunning beauty that emerges from the same simple equation. You can use a more complicated equation, but you don't get a more complicated result, just a different one.

Further, even though we start graphing fractals one point at a time, after they have become graphs, the individual points each become their own universe of points, something you can fully realize only by watching an animation. Zoom in on any one point, and you'll find that it is not a point but a galaxy and then a cosmos of points, each one of which in turn is its own cosmos, each cosmos a tiny replica of the original, but not so much a carbon copy, boring in its similarity, but with a beauty that is constantly being enriched by both its similarity to the whole and its own uniqueness.

This is another emergent quality to fractals: it is only when the fractal as a collection of points is graphed that the true nature of the fractal emerges from the collective of the whole. It is the interaction between the equation and the graph that allows the full relationship to be revealed.

Much of a fractal is empty space; in fact, you could say that since individual points have no real dimension, there is nothing in a fractal but vast amounts of empty space with an occasional point that really isn't there anyway; very much like space itself.

And again, when all of these things that aren't there are collected and viewed from a distance, in very much a quantum sort of way, something emerges that is a complex interplay and interweaving of space and points into an emergent beauty and elegance that is far more than just the sum of its parts. Each point has a vital role to play, each point its own cosmos, but no point has any role to play in isolation, outside of the relationship they all have together, an emergent relationship that is defined purely by the relationship itself. Each point's role is defined by the original equation, its value coming from outside itself, with no apparent value in and of itself, but with transcendent value as a part of the whole.

Thus has God put the universe together.

What you ought to tell me at this point is that you've never heard of fractals, and even if you have, they are just interesting little curious mathematical anomalies that have no meaning for most of humanity. Math geeks can get all excited, but that's why we call them "geeks." They get excited over pointless graphs. At best, fractals would make cool T-shirts.

To which we will respond, the title of this chapter is "Fractalated Universe." It seems very much as though the template for the universe and everything in it might be fractals, from very small and insignificant things to the largest of objects in the universe, from sunflowers and ferns to coastlines to galaxies, clusters of galaxies, and super-clusters of galaxies, self-similarity pops up in all kinds of unexpected places.

Rather than rewrite the sections that talk about this in *Life, the Universe, and Everything*, let's look at a progression of breathtaking fractals done by Roger Johnston and used with his permission, taken from the following website: http://community.webshots.com/user/rajahh/ :

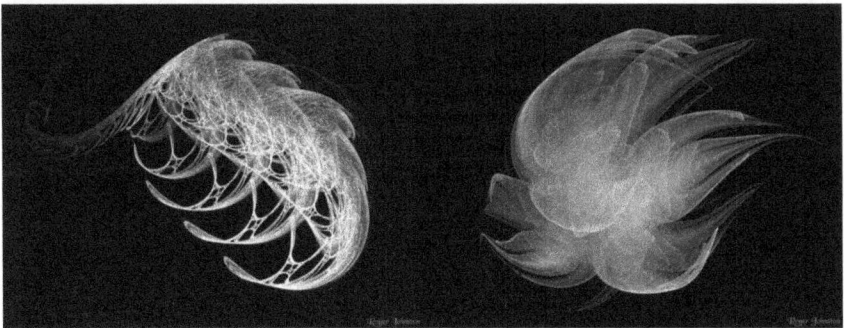

Johnston colored these, presumably using software to do so, but the images themselves are fractals with no more complicated an origin than any other fractal, $y=z^2+c$. Feel free to do your own research into fractals—nothing could be easier on the Internet than to Google the word *fractal* to see what you get. Try "fractal life"—that works well. If you see echoes of living things in many of Johnston's images, it's not coincidence, nor is it just art imitating life. Fractal life is not just found in fractal images—life seems to be fractalated in ways that reveal themselves the more you investigate, and not just life, but the structure of the universe.

And so, Jesus. On the face of it, just another poor baby without even the good fortune to be born in his own home, one more pointless child in a world of pointless poor children, with no potential for transcendent significance, very little hope of survival, living in a backwater part of a backwater world in a backwater solar system in a backwater galaxy in a pointless universe. You don't to have to go very far away from earth before it becomes just a point, and not far beyond that before it fades away altogether.

Just to illustrate that point, there's a view of Saturn's rings taken by Cassini—the tiny dot above the rings is earth. Not much further than that, the sun becomes a dot and then vanishes. Then the Milky Way itself becomes a dot, one more inconsequential galaxy in a sea of 200 billion galaxies. Most of the stars you see on an unusually clear night from a high mountain are in fact galaxies, or so I have been told, and most of the many billions of galaxies, with their many billions of stars, you can't see at all, not even as tiny dots in space.

So why would this Jesus baby matter?

Yes, of course, son of God, virgin birth, messiah, death, resurrection, all that.

But, really, so what? We need some context. See if this works.

Jesus is the finite representation of the infinite God, and of course when we say infinite, we mean outside of space-time. Jesus is God in space-time, a four-dimensional fractal of the outside-of-four-dimensional God. As any point of a fractal is the same as every point of the fractal, so is every point of Jesus the same as every point of God, and yet, a point of the fractal is not the whole fractal, and so Jesus is not all of God. He is the same as God, but he does not show us all of God, except that everything he shows us is exactly as God is. When we see a piece of the fractal, we both see the whole fractal, and only a tiny part of the fractal, all at once, and when we see Jesus, we see all of God, and only the part of God that fits into four-dimensions.

Jesus starts from the simplest of points, from a human egg nudged by the Butterfly's wing into fertilization, a tiny touch from the infinite God, a point too small to see, and then, as with all of us, every cell that develops is exactly the same as every other cell, its DNA identical, but every cell is differentiated into a different form, all the same, all different, all man, all God. Even as humans, we are fractals.

As we have seen, the tiniest of points in our universe is what makes everything happen, and this tiniest of points, this egg, this zygote, this embryo, this fetus, this infant, this toddler, this child and teen and adult, this tiniest of points contained within it everything of God and everything of man, the relationship between the two realized and bridged in the most elegant and beautiful of ways, from the simplest of things, no more than an egg, to the most complex, the infinite God, all contained, self-similar, infinite and finite all at once.

Some have trouble with the Trinity within Christianity, this weirdo three-in-one thing that makes no sense in a world that is, as we now know, enslaved by a mechanistic, reductionist mindset. The quantum has no problem with three-in-one, of course, and now with Chaos and fractals, we see that three is contained within one, the same as the one, and yet different, all part of the same, but each with its own flavor. The bits of the fractal emerge from within the fractal, as Jesus from God, as the Holy Spirit from God, different and the same.

Is God in fact infinite? He is infinite in that he is outside of space and time, but there is no infinity in a universe with a starting point in space and time. In a quantum universe, there is no infinitely small. There is only as small as we are allowed to get, and no smaller.

But in a fractalated universe, there is infinity within the fractal.

Chapter 12

Fractal Jesus

Relax. It's just a fractal. Those aren't hands.

But if they were, would they be hands reaching out for help from the dark abyss of the soul? Or would they be hands reaching out to help, each isolated hand being given strength and influence because of the infinity of hands inside it? Or if they are reaching out for help, are they prevented from escape by the infinitely heavy drag of infinitely many hands dragging it back, each tiny hand with almost no influence at all, but all of the hands together forming a gravitational black hole of despair, all being dragged into an event horizon of infinite emptiness where time and space cease to exist altogether? Are they hands with questions, or with answers?

It is, regardless, an infinity of hands, not just those we can see, but an infinity of hands we cannot see, each an identical part of the whole, each with its own little bit of difference, of individuality, and as we know, it is the little differences that make all the difference.

Roger Johnston

Sunrise or sunset? Light overcoming the darkness, or darkness overcoming the light? Big Bang, or Black Hole? Fractal heaven and its portals, or fractal hell and its demons? Either way, the infinity awaits.

We are all fractals of something. Our free will lets each one of us have his or her own little piece of individuality, that little bit that makes all the difference, but we are none of us anything at all without the whole to which we belong. I suppose we get to choose that to which we belong, and then we become a little fractalated piece of its fractal.

I choose to be part of the fractal Jesus.

It was, and remains, Jesus' role to bridge the infinite gap between God and man, to show man the character of God. It is, and remains, our role to bridge the gap between Jesus and mankind, to show mankind the character of Jesus, and thus the character of God.

We could try to do it on our own, making up our own rules and regulations as we go along, but then, one could say, we have chosen our own starting values for z and c, and even though the equation remains the same in its simplicity, it is the tiny variations in the starting values that make all the difference. We may get nothing at all, no fractal, no rhyme nor reason to life, nothing but randomness and pointless indifference (literally pointless, since we would have no fractal), or we might get a wildly different fractal that is not the fractal Jesus.

I'm really going to stretch to reach the point here, just for fun. There are just two values needed to generate the fractal, one each for z and c. There are just two tiny variations in the early universe that gave rise to all the order and structure of the universe—a $1/100,000^{th}$ of a degree difference in the background microwave radiation, and a 1 in a billion chance that particles would arrive without their antiparticles. There are two elements to the path that the universe took —particles and forces. There are two things that the universe is composed of—space-time and matter. Energy divided itself into two things—positive energy (matter) and negative energy (gravity).

Each one of these then heads down a fractal path, and I've probably grossly oversimplified things just to get to where I want to go.

But there are two things that we are supposed to do to be fractal Jesuses: Love God, and love each other. And just like everything else, all the rest of life, the laws, the rules and regulations, everything else should come from these two. As everything comes from the interactions between particles and forces, between matter and gravity, between the hot spots and the cold spots in space, as the tiny little bits of matter and the interactions between them defined the rest of history, so these two little rules define what it means to be a fractal Jesus.

As Jesus is a fractal bit of God, the finite representation of the infinite God, so am I supposed to be a fractal bit of Jesus. I am different in tiny, seemingly unimportant ways from Jesus, as I am from everyone else who has ever lived, and those ways define the uniqueness of my life and existence, but I am supposed to be like Jesus in every way.

As you look at any piece of any fractal at any magnification, whether at 1900 or 169 quintillion times smaller than the original, and find the original, so you are to look at me and find Jesus. I am unimaginably smaller than the original, yet I am meant to be the original in the way that I live my life.

You don't have to understand all of this fractal stuff to get that.

But that doesn't mean that it's easy to get.

All through Christian history, Christians have been trying to be like little Jesuses, and instead we end up, as it were, finding our own values for z and c and creating our own little fractal universes that most often stray from the Fractal Jesus. It is our curse and our virtue, I guess, that we want to do things our own way, and the truth is, fractals are complex, and so is Jesus, not even to mention the complexity of God.

Since it's impossible to understand God without understanding Jesus, and since it seems to be pretty impossible to understand Jesus, we grab a piece of the fractal and try to live in that universe. The 2008 Olympics in Beijing is happening as I write this. A young American wrestler is quoted in the paper as saying, "I don't want to tread the path everybody else has. I want to make a name for myself."[75] He is all of us.

It might be the healing piece, or the speaking-in-tongues bit, or the abundant life bit, or the being-angry-at-the-Pharisees bit (which usually turns into just being angry at whomever), or grace and mercy, or judgment and wrath, or getting lots of talents (that is, money and goodies), or helping the poor and cursing the rich, or (I'm not sure where we find this one, frankly) helping the rich and cursing the poor, or enforcing the law, or overthrowing the government, or killing the pagans (who are generally those who get in the way of where we want to go), and the list goes on.

It might also be a Buddhist fractal, or Muslim or Jewish or Hindu. It might be a hedonist or Druid or agnostic or atheist fractal, or a drugs, sex and rock and roll fractal.

It might be a science or math fractal, or writing or painting or living under a bridge, or the reason and skepticism fractal.

We will all become part of something greater than ourselves, and we become fractalated, a smaller part of that whole that resembles the whole in many ways. Even the rugged individualists fractalate; I don't want to hurt anyone's feelings here, but all Harley riders look alike. Before you beat me to death with a, I don't know, pick the Harley part or tool of choice here, recognize that each part of the fractal is different, but each is similar to the whole. It is our human nature to want to be different enough to be different, but not so different that we are actually, you know, different. We want to be different within the fractal we have chosen, but similar to the fractal. We want to belong, purely and simply, and we will do what it takes to belong, because in belonging, we find our value as human beings.

But there is no value at all unless God is in the fractal. I might even be willing to go as far as to suggest that without God, the values you choose for z and c will not give you a fractal at all. Your graph will diverge into nothingness.

I can only quote Richard Dawkins first on this topic, as we did in the first book: The universe "has precisely the properties we should expect if there is, at bottom, no design, no purpose, no evil and no good, nothing but pointless indifference"; human beings are "machines for propagating DNA."[76]

Stephen Weinberg can defend me again on this point of pointlessness:

---

[75] 18-year-old Jake Deitchler, in The Denver Post, 12 Aug 2008, pp 2c
[76] Richard Dawkins, *The Selfish Gene*

The more the universe seems comprehensible, the more it seems pointless. . . . At the other end of the spectrum are the opponents of reductionism who are appalled by what they feel to be the bleakness of modern science. To whatever extent they and their world can be reduced to a matter of particles or fields and their interactions, they feel diminished by that knowledge. I would not try to answer these critics with a pep talk about the beauties of modern science. The reductionist worldview is chilling and impersonal. It has to be accepted as it is, not because we like it, but because that is the way the world works.[77]

And Francis Crick, co-discoverer of DNA: "Your joys and sorrows, your memories and ambitions, your sense of personal identity and free will are in fact no more than the behavior of a vast assembly of nerve cells and their associated molecules."[78]

I have a young atheist friend whom I shall call Troy who talked with me not too long ago about what we might call his existential crisis: in our conversations together (and it was all my fault), he had come to realize that unless God exists, he had no way to find any meaning or purpose to his life. He had become intellectually suicidal, which is to be differentiated from being emotionally suicidal; being intellectually suicidal doesn't often lead to suicide, just to despair and finally into some other sort of delusion.

Troy and I decided that this was another, more sophisticated form of Pascal's Wager. In its original form, or at least as it has been popularized and criticized, the Wager is that you might as well believe in God. If you don't, and he exists, then you go to hell. If you do, and he doesn't, then you've lost nothing.

In Troy's case, it's not so much arriving in heaven or hell that is the issue; it's what to do in the interim. If you are going to find meaning and purpose in your life, then it only has transcendent meaning and purpose if God exists. Otherwise, regardless of what you decide to focus your existence on, it is a delusional meaning, a fraudulent purpose. Troy cannot force himself to believe in God, and thus he finds himself in an awkward position; he must commit himself to living a life without purpose.

The thinking works like this. Steven Weinberg makes this statement: "Though aware that there is nothing in the universe that suggests any purpose for humanity, one way that we can find a purpose is to study the universe by the

---

[77] Stephen Weinberg, *Dreams of a Final Theory*
[78] Francis Crick, *The Astonishing Hypothesis: The Scientific Search for the Soul*

methods of science, without consoling ourselves with fairy tales about its future, or about our own."[79]

Any attempt one makes to give one's life meaning is a fairy tale, notwithstanding Dr. Weinberg's assertion that spending a lifetime studying the universe has meaning. We would call that the "Science Delusion," which will travel on the same train with the Art Delusion, the Acting Delusion, the Politics Delusion, the Philanthropy Delusion, the Religion Delusion, the Drugs, Sex and Rock & Roll Delusion, the Harley Delusion, the Getting Rich and Staying Rich Delusion, the Minimalist Delusion, and the Everybody Else Is an Idiot Delusion.

If I seem to be taking a dig at Richard Dawkins for his book *The God Delusion*, that would be accurate. If God exists, then there is only one non-delusional way to live. If he does not exist, then everything is a delusion. In fact, as we have seen, even reality itself, as Einstein pointed out, is a delusion, since we are formed of particles that aren't really here.

So as Troy observed, from his point of view we are each forced to commit intellectual suicide in order to live, and all forms of intellectual suicide are equally invalid. Either we will choose the God Delusion or we will choose some other Delusion. One way or the other, we will have to fool ourselves into living our lives, since the only meaning we can have will be meaning that we create like a Halloween costume, only without as much basis in reality.

As I was typing the previous sentence, I misspelled the word as *Holloween*. That's what our lives will be, hollow and echoing on the inside, covered by a thin sheen of pretense, threatened at any moment to have it ripped away and the fraud exposed, if not in life, then finally in death.

That is, if God does not exist. I maintain that the God of Relativity, the Quantum God, the Chaos and Complex God does exist, that the universe reveals his existence, that we are to follow the Fractal Jesus, and that is because he is so beautiful, so elegant, so simple and complex, so easy and impossible to understand, so normal and so mysterious, so natural and so miraculous, and because he has given us the choice and the evidence to follow him. Either they are all Delusions, or one of them isn't, and the only one that has the potential of being Not A Delusion is the God option. I'll take that bet, not on the basis of Pascal's wager, but on the weight of the scientific evidence in its favor.

There was a brief report on National Public Radio about a kids camp for skeptics, for kids who don't believe in God and don't follow a religion:

---

[79] Steven Weinberg, The New York Review of Books, quoted in the New York Times, 1 Jan 2002, *The Universe Might Last Forever, Astronomers Say, but Life Might Not,* by Dennis Overbyte

> Cilone speaks up. "I call myself a Christian," he says, "but if I get proof that there is no God and Christianity is a wild goose chase, then I would completely abandon it."
>
> Sutherland rushes to assure him, there is no God.
>
> "If God really, really wanted us to know he existed, he'd make daily appearances: Like 'It's 3:15. Oh, it's God time!'"

When old-fashioned, outdated but still-in-use science is used to convince kids and adults of all ages that there is no real evidence of God, that the only evidence for his existence that you could believe would be his physical self appearing on stage nightly for a bit of God stand-up, it is an intellectual, academic and scientific tragedy. We think in terms of "proof," not in terms of "evidence." Earlier in the show, this interchange took place:

> As 12-year-old Chloe Morgan gazes at the stars, she says she does not see the handiwork of God. "It seems kind of like an accident almost, like the Big Bang that created the universe was an accident," Morgan says. "It was a beautiful mistake or something."

We want proof for God's existence, and we deny the power of the evidence. But as soon as God appears and claims to be God, does great works and miracles to demonstrate to us that he is in fact God, criticizes all the hyperreligious people for their intolerance and cruelty, establishes reasonable rules for behavior, and gives us morals and ethics that make sense and are easy to interpret, then we reject him because he is not God the way we conceive of God to be, and we put him on a cross and watch him die, now convinced that because we have killed him, he was not God at all.

The NPR interviewer asked the kids a question. She said, Most people believe in God because they are afraid of death, afraid of not existing. Do you kids worry about that? (The on-air question was slightly differently worded.)

> But what about the afterlife? Are these kids comfortable with the idea that when people die, that's it?
>
> "It's a scary thought, not existing. But it's not anything I can stop, so I'm going to use what time I have to do everything I can and would like to do," Lee says.

> The group falls silent as 15-year-old Jared Nauman, one of the quieter but more confirmed atheists in the group, speaks for the first time.
>
> "I'm terrified of not existing," Nauman says, his voice shaking. "I'm kind of stuck there. I don't know what else to think."
>
> A long pause ensues, broken by Grothe.
>
> "Yeah, but here you all are, skeptical of the afterlife, but you're not sitting in a room obsessed with it. You're at Camp Inquiry, having fun," he says.
>
> His words hang in the air for five long seconds.
>
> "Until now!" someone says, and they begin to laugh.
>
> After a few more moments, the campers stop pondering the meaning of life and death, and move onto the next important task at hand: hurling water balloons with as much force as Newton's laws of motion allow.[80]

The moment was over. There is no evidence for God, no need for God. Even a child can see that. It's the Fun Delusion; the fun that we can have at this moment will hide the reality of the future from us. It is childlike and sweet to hide from the terrors of life and death and reality at camp having fun, but it is tragic and pointless to spend a life in hiding, unless of course that is the only option.

And without God, there are no other options. There are only delusions. Pick your own. There are no wrong choices, or perhaps it's better to say, there are no right choices. Camp Inquiry would like its little campers to choose to be skeptical, reasonable, irreligious, moral and ethical beings concerned, one would guess, with being tolerant of others, careful with the environment, and concerned with human rights. All of these are excellent choices, if there is a God, but if not, then they hold no more or less value than genocide, homicide, or suicide.

For if there is no God, there is no value. As Dawkins says with the courage of his convictions as a scientific atheist, "There's no design, no purpose, no evil and no good, nothing but pointless indifference." Wienberg matches him with, "there is nothing in the universe that suggests any purpose for humanity." In *Pale Blue Dot* (earth from a distance), Carl Sagan adds, "Our posturings, our imagined self-importance, the delusion that we have some privileged position in the Universe, are challenged by this point of pale light." The universe itself

---

[80] **Camp Offers Training Ground For Little Skeptics,** by Barbara Bradley Hagerty, *All Things Considered*, 7 Aug 2008, www.npr.org/templates/story/story.php?storyId=93174374

doesn't matter; how much less earth, and you and I are not even worth considering.

In this view, matter may matter in a physical sense, but matter matters not at all in a metaphysical sense. It as, as Weinberg describes it above, just "a matter of particles or fields and their interactions." That is the sum total of the universe.

That's all it does. There is nothing more.

Chapter 13
It's God Time

"If God really, really wanted us to know he existed, he'd make daily appearances: Like 'It's 3:15. Oh, it's God time!'"

But of course, he did show up and make an appearance, all day every day for thirty-three years. Or not, depending on what you believe, and that of course would be true for the young person behind that quote. It's the difference between evidence and proof. There is no proof in science, only varying degrees of evidence, from no evidence whatsoever to overwhelming evidence, but as all good scientists know, even overwhelming evidence can turn out, on the basis of further evidence, to be overwhelmingly wrong.

We bandy the word *proof* around in science as though it has meaning, but it's a sloppy usage of an imprecise word. Up until 1975, we could identify and describe physically 100 percent of everything in the universe. By 1998, what used to be 100% of everything in the universe was now 4%. We have no idea how to talk about 96% of the stuff in the universe other than to give it a couple of names, Dark Energy* and Dark Matter*. We know they must be there, but we don't know what they are.

And then we demand proof of God's existence, when we should know better. There is just evidence, and the existence of free will (which is open to debate, as well) means that we can accept or reject evidence as we will. We can accept lousy evidence, we can reject overwhelming evidence, and we tend to do both not on the basis of logic or reason, but on our personal inclinations. We justify our beliefs, or lack of beliefs, using logic, reason, faith, evidence, experience, historicity, and whatever, but for any of us to be pressed into admitting why we believe or disbelieve will always come down to personal choice.

Even our ability to reason is colored by the culture of our intellect. As we make decisions based on the culture we live in, and those decisions are based on unconscious cultural assumptions, so we reason from the unconscious background of our intellectual landscape, driven by assumptions we do not know we are making. Little Chloe Morgan from above, all of 12 years old, said as she was gazing at the stars in the night sky that "It seems kind of like an accident almost, like the Big Bang that created the universe was an accident. It was a beautiful mistake or something." She knows nothing of Big Bang, nothing of science's rejection of Big Bang because it seemed too much like religion, nothing of the nothingness, the Singularity, the arrival of space-time and the laws of physics. She is almost empty of real knowledge of Big Bang, and on that basis, rejects the existence of God. Even the word *beautiful* has no meaning outside the existence of God except as we choose to define it for ourselves.

It would be unfair to pick on Chloe, since she is so young, since she has been told about these things by most modern scientists who seem, as a group, to have forgotten how much Big Bang sounded like the first chapter of Genesis. They now embrace it as evidence that God does not exist. We have given them enough ammunition that if they can find evidence that something happened according to the laws of nature (which, by the way, doesn't fit Big Bang, but let's not quibble), then God is dealt out of the picture. Any natural explanation precludes the supernatural, and thus there is no God. Russian leader Nikita Khrushchev famously said, "(Yuri) Gagarin flew into space, but didn't see any God there."[81] It is not just 12-year-olds who build belief systems based on foolish observations, especially since Gagarin himself believed in God despite not having had a face-to-face conversation with him in his brief time in space.

This is our fault as believers. We have somehow, as we have said, reduced God to being the God of the supernatural and eliminated the God of the natural. We have conditioned the nonbelievers to look for God in the supernatural, not in nature itself except for the odd rainbow and sunset, and maybe at childbirth, but we talk constantly about "miracles" as though there is nothing natural about God. For nonbelievers, there is no God because there is nothing supernatural, and thus there is no place for God in the natural. Chloe "does not see the handiwork of God" in the stars, because they are natural, not supernatural, and so there is no place for God to be.

It is perhaps time for us to consider the natural God, the God who created nature and all of its rules, laws, and forces, as being the same as the supernatural, miraculous God. It's hard to say what impact this will have on our understanding of God, but it will not be negligible. We need to reconcile the God of the Bible with the God of our experience, and we will enter here into a struggle together. I know this to be true because it is a struggle within me, and I have not yet reached reconciliation.

Let's create the tension:

First, the Bible is full of miracles, full of moments when God intervenes into the lives of people, peoples, and nations. It's not just Jesus who does miracles, and it's not just in the New Testament. Creation seems miraculous, and then we have all kinds of things going on: floods and arks, towers and languages, plagues and water-parting and rescues, manna and water from rocks, healing snakes, tablets on mountain tops, pillars of salt and flames from heaven, wrestling angels, and the list goes on and on.

---

[81] Answers.com, www.answers.com/topic/yuri-gagarin#wp-_note-4

God's contact with his people seems clearly to have been demonstrated miraculously as the main way God works. As much as Thomas Jefferson and many others have been made uncomfortable by the miracles in scripture and tried to get rid of them (because miracles can't have happened and make our faith seem unintelligent), the greatest miracle of all, the resurrection, is the linchpin to our faith and cannot be denied without destroying the faith altogether.

We also see miracles after the Ascension; in the early church, in the lives of Peter, Paul and the disciples/apostles, and these lead us to believe, along with the clear words of Jesus, that we can expect the miraculous in our lives and ministries, in our own walks of faith. There will be healings and miraculous gifts that will build the kingdom. We were told that we can do more even than was done in the Bible, and we have the expectation that this will be true.

Bottom line: when given the choice between ordinary and miraculous, to us God seems to default to the miraculous as the best way to build his kingdom. Witness Jesus when questioned about the healing of the blind man in John 9:

> As he went along, he saw a man blind from birth. His disciples asked him, "Rabbi, who sinned, this man or his parents, that he was born blind?" "Neither this man nor his parents sinned," said Jesus, "but this happened so that the work of God might be displayed in his life. As long as it is day, we must do the work of him who sent me. Night is coming, when no one can work. While I am in the world, I am the light of the world."[82]

The work of Jesus, and of all of us fractal Jesuses, is to display the work of God in our lives, to build the kingdom of God.

Miracles demonstrate the reality of God as different from the norm, more powerful than the norm. Miracles, purely and simply, are hard to ignore, though not impossible, as we know:

> Jesus stepped into a boat, crossed over and came to his own town. Some men brought to him a paralytic, lying on a mat. When Jesus saw their faith, he said to the paralytic, "Take heart, son; your sins are forgiven." At this, some of the teachers of the law said to themselves, "This fellow is blaspheming!" Knowing their thoughts, Jesus said, "Why do you entertain evil thoughts in your hearts? Which is easier: to

---

[82] John 9:1-5 (NIV)

say, 'Your sins are forgiven,' or to say, 'Get up and walk'? But so that you may know that the Son of Man has authority on earth to forgive sins...." Then he said to the paralytic, "Get up, take your mat and go home." And the man got up and went home. When the crowd saw this, they were filled with awe; and they praised God, who had given such authority to men.[83]

The true miracle was the forgiveness of sins; it's worth remembering that the goal of miracles is to validate salvation, not to make us feel better; that is, it is the purpose of miracles to build the kingdom. The secondary miracle in this story was getting up, taking the mat, and going home, but that was the hard-to-ignore miracle that validated the easier-to-ignore, harder-to-do miracle—the forgiveness of sins.

But not impossible to ignore: "Then some of the Pharisees and teachers of the law said to him, 'Teacher, we want to see a miraculous sign from you.'"[84] They had already seen the miracles; "God time" was all around them, but they wanted God on demand, their way, their timing, their understanding of who they thought the Messiah was supposed to be. As do we all. Would they have believed any miracle? I'm thinking, not.

"And he did not do many miracles there because of their lack of faith."[85] I wonder what this means for us.

Because, second, we live in a time of few miracles. We hear claims for miracles, we hear demands for miracles as proof that God exists ("If God really, really wanted us to know he existed, he'd make daily appearances: Like 'It's 3:15. Oh, it's God time!'"), we hear denials of miracles from the world of science, and many of us are skeptical of all the claims. Why? For most of us, it is because we have not seen for ourselves, and perhaps we would not believe if we did.

Science has disproved miracles too many times for us to be able to ignore, has found explanations that are too reasonable, and so in the face of another miracle we cannot explain, we expect that science will explain it one day. Carl Sagan's son Nick said it for all of science: "There are no miracles. Not for you, certainly not for me. Not for any of us."[86] Interestingly, his father, in a speech in front of the Cathedral of St. John the Divine in New York in 1995 and after surviving a life-threatening illness, made this comment: "I would like to thank from the bottom of my heart the fact that people in this congregation, so many

---

[83] Matt 9:1-8 (NIV)
[84] Matt 12:38 (NIV)
[85] Matt 13:58 (NIV)
[86] Goodreads review by Jessica, www.goodreads.com/review/show/1511078

of them produced prayers and good wishes for my health and survival, I'm deeply grateful and while I think it would be too much to say that it worked, the net result is that I seem to be fully recovered."[87] Evidence is, of course, not proof.

Many no longer believe in physical healing; too many times, the healings have not been proven, or they can be ascribed to something else. Many may feel that the body has resources for healing that science does not yet understand, and they are loathe to play God-of-the-gaps one more time. The world, after all, is not flat. There are too many charlatans in churches and on TV, faking healings to make money, so that it is hard to distinguish the *faux* from the *vrai*. We have been trained to be skeptics, to use our minds, and to reject the miraculous as, again, the province of the primitive and superstitious, the ignorant and deceived.

Third, our prayers for miracles go unanswered, unheeded. We try to cut God a little slack to give him a break, but scripture tells us that he will hear our prayers, and so we expect him to do so. When terrible things happen to loved ones or friends, or to cities or countries, and though we pray, nothing is changed, then we have no answers to offer other than to point to the mysterious ways of the unknowable God. We Christians become like Muslims and Hindus, blaming the bad on the will of God, no different from saying "inshallah" or "karma"; that is, it's just God's will, always God's will, never not God's will, and it's your own fault. A friend told me today that God had given her cancer so that she could learn through the process. I've had four friends die of cancer in the past two years, and I'm not sure that what they learned was all that useful to them.

God does not give anyone cancer. God does not take infants by death, nor fathers nor mothers nor boys nor girls. God does not cause earthquakes nor tornadoes, nor does he "allow" them to happen, as though using the word *allow* would absolve him of blame. God did not cause AIDS to kill millions and orphan millions of others. He does not cause car wrecks, plane crashes, boat sinkings, homicide, genocide, suicide, bridge collapses, hurricanes, tornadoes, tsunamis, avalanches, floods, droughts, pimples, or migraines.

There's a problem with that paragraph above, which might continue on for pages and pages of all the disasters and tragedies that befall us. We can find God doing similar things in the Bible. So we could make a case that he does cause all those things and more. In fact, if we want the Bible to tell us that God is responsible for all the miracles we perceive around us, then we are forced to give him responsibility for all of the terrible things that happen, as well. And frankly, he may be. As Job said to his wife, "Shall we accept good from God

---

[87] SETI Carl Sagan Speech from 1995, http://seti.sentry.net/archive/public/1999/5-99/00000351.htm

and not trouble?" The Bible itself allows us to give God the credit for the good and to take the blame for the bad.

And that's why many many people reject the idea of God. A God that orchestrates a history of human pain and suffering for his own mysterious purposes is not the God they want to worship. Many of the mighty works of God in scripture were terrible—as he promised his people in 2 Kings: "Therefore this is what the Lord, the God of Israel, says: I am going to bring such disaster on Jerusalem and Judah that the ears of everyone who hears of it will tingle."[88] He promised prosperity for the people if they were obedient, and disaster if they were not. As they leaned heavily toward disobedience, disaster was normative, and it came as a result of sin by the people (just do a word search on a Bible website using the word *disaster* to discover it for yourself). God punished his people regularly and harshly, most often to the point of just preserving a remnant to keep his people going.

This is not often considered part of our modern western theology. Remember the harsh and condemning reaction by many to Reverend Jeremiah Wright's sermon when, as recorded by *ABC News*, he thundered,

> "No, no, no, God damn America, that's in the Bible for killing innocent people," he said in a 2003 sermon. "God damn America for treating our citizens as less than human. God damn America for as long as she acts like she is God and she is supreme."
>
> In addition to damning America, he told his congregation on the Sunday after Sept. 11, 2001 that the United States had brought on al Qaeda's attacks because of its own terrorism.
>
> "We bombed Hiroshima, we bombed Nagasaki, and we nuked far more than the thousands in New York and the Pentagon, and we never batted an eye," Rev. Wright said in a sermon on Sept. 16, 2001.
>
> "We have supported state terrorism against the Palestinians and black South Africans, and now we are indignant because the stuff we have done overseas is now brought right back to our own front yards. America's chickens are coming home to roost," he told his congregation.[89]

---

[88] 2 Kings 21:12 (NIV)

[89] **Obama's Pastor: God Damn America, U.S. to Blame for 9/11,** By BRIAN ROSS and REHAB EL-BURI, March 13, 2008, ABC News, http://abcnews.go.com/Blotter/Story?id=4443788

Whether or not one agrees with the history and the sentiment, it is consonant with disaster theology as found in scripture, only in the Bible, God is punishing his own people, not some random country 4000 years later.

To recap: we have reduced God to being that God who blesses us when we pray and fast, and we have no real understanding of the God who punishes. But in Isaiah 58, the prophet writes for God when he says,

> 'Shout it aloud, do not hold back. Raise your voice like a trumpet. Declare to my people their rebellion and to the house of Jacob their sins. For day after day they seek me out; they seem eager to know my ways, as if they were a nation that does what is right and has not forsaken the commands of its God. They ask me for just decisions and seem eager for God to come near them. 'Why have we fasted,' they say, 'and you have not seen it? Why have we humbled ourselves, and you have not noticed?' Yet on the day of your fasting, you do as you please and exploit all your workers. Your fasting ends in quarreling and strife, and in striking each other with wicked fists. You cannot fast as you do today and expect your voice to be heard on high. Is this the kind of fast I have chosen, only a day for a man to humble himself? Is it only for bowing one's head like a reed and for lying on sackcloth and ashes? Is that what you call a fast, a day acceptable to the Lord ? Is not this the kind of fasting I have chosen: to loose the chains of injustice and untie the cords of the yoke, to set the oppressed free and break every yoke? Is it not to share your food with the hungry and to provide the poor wanderer with shelter—when you see the naked, to clothe him, and not to turn away from your own flesh and blood?"[90]

So now we have a choice to make: we ascribe to God *all the good* and *all the evil* that exists, because we cannot do one without the other, not if we want the Bible to be true in the way we'd like for it to be true, the way in which we have reduced it. Though it may sound ridiculous or terrible to say it, if God answers our prayers for good things, then he also punishes us for bad things, and all the bad things that happen to people are punishment in one form or another, whether it is the loss of a newborn, a hurricane that destroys a city, or a tsunami that devastates countries and takes a quarter of a million lives.

Everything happens for a reason, God is in charge, and therefore everything that happens, happens because he wills it. There are no other options.

Or we come to a new understanding of God and how he works in his universe.

---

[90] Isaiah 58: 1-7 (NIV)

Glossary of Terms as they appear in Chapter Thirteen

Dark Energy – We're not going to beat this to death with details. In 1998, it was discovered that the universe was expanding more rapidly than it should have been. It should have been slowing down, but it was speeding up. It's like this: you ride your bike or skateboard down a hill and then head up a hill on the other side. What should happen is that you will gradually slow down – maybe you reach the top, maybe you stop in the middle of the hill. Likewise, our universe, after the big push of Big Bang, should have been slowing down, but somehow, it wasn't. This is like you on your bike or skateboard in the middle of the hill you are going up, gradually slowing, until suddenly you speed up, accelerate. What does it take for that to happen? It takes energy. So the universe needs some extra energy boost to begin accelerating its expansion. So what do you call energy that you can't see? Well, it's dark, since we can't see it, and it's energy, so we'll call it Dark Energy. It has to be there, it has to be just over 74% of everything in the universe, but we can't find it and don't know what it is.

Dark Matter – We're not going to beat this to death with details. In 1933, a Swiss astronomer named Fritz Zwicky at Cal Tech discovered that galaxies were spinning around too fast to be able to be held together by the matter that was in them. In fact, you needed about five times as much matter as was visible in a galaxy to keep it from spinning itself apart. So the matter had to be there, but we couldn't see it. What do you call matter you can't see? Well, it's dark, and it's matter, so we'll call it Dark Matter. Nobody paid any attention to Fritz because he was really irritating and hard to get along with. In 1975, astronomer Vera Rubin announced similar observations, and after a lot of controversy, she was believed. Dark matter is just under 22% of everything in the universe, but we can't find it and don't know what it is.

What's left – ordinary matter and stellar gas. Stellar gas is about 3.6% of what's in the universe, so ordinary ("baryonic") matter, all the stuff that you and I are made of and that we can see around us on earth and in the night sky, is about .4% of everything that exists in the universe. Now that's depressing. And, in the latest news, about half of that is now missing. Swell.

Chapter 14
Order out of Chaos

There's something we need to admit right up front—we can't reconcile God, the Bible and science completely. I'm not sure why that's a problem, though I know why we *think* it's a problem.

The intense debate between science and religion oscillates around an assumption being made by both science and religion, as we discussed earlier—that is, that science is finished with itself and has decided, on the basis of what science knows about the universe right now, that there is no God, no evidence to be found of God in science. For science, that is supposed to be the end of the argument. Right now at this moment, there is no evidence for God, and there never will be. God and science live in separate neighborhoods and need to stay there, because science is for intelligent people who base their beliefs on evidence, not on superstition, which is what religious people do.

Religion's fairly lame response (if there's anything we're really good at, it's lame responses) to this has been to attack what science knows, trying to show that it isn't true, and we hardly present a united front. Some argue about the age of the universe, cherry-picking evidence to "prove" their point. Most try to prove that evolution is wrong, again trying to find evidence in science that God did everything as Genesis 1 records it. Some try to reconcile traditional neo-Darwinian evolution with their faith, most notably Francis Collins of the Human Genome Project, along with a small number of believers who accept evolution as it stands and try to make it fit with the faith. The Intelligent Design folks do a better job of dealing with more modern science but make the mistake of using the word "Design," which implies blueprints and a grand, specific plan for everything to have been designed by God exactly the way that it is, and they still spend most of their time arguing about evolution.

The most compelling is the Fine Tuning group, led unofficially by Hugh Ross and his team, finding in the tight parameters under which the universe operates an unlikely mix of physical conditions that seems carefully orchestrated to allow the universe to produce what it has produced, especially humans. A attack on Fine Tuning in *NewScientist* by Fred Adams at the University of Michigan twiddles with the knobs a bit to suggest that the argument doesn't carry the strength we might hope for, but he has to create other universes in the process,[91] something increasingly easy for scientists to do even in the face of a complete lack of evidence that other universes exist.

However, another article posits that:

---

[91] **In the multiverse, stars burn black**, Michael Brooks, NewScientist, 2 Aug 2008, pp. 10

prevailing theoretical models attempting to explain the formation of the solar system have assumed it to be average in every way. Now a new study by Northwestern University astronomers, using recent data from the 300 exoplanets discovered orbiting other stars, turns that view on its head. The solar system, it turns out, is pretty special indeed. The study illustrates that if early conditions had been just slightly different, very unpleasant things could have happened—like planets being thrown into the sun or jettisoned into deep space.[92]

A third article states that

Earth is one special planet. It has liquid water, plate tectonics, and an atmosphere that shelters it from the worst of the sun's rays. But many scientists agree our planet's most special feature might just be us. "Without water the planet would be geologically dead," said Caltech's Mike Brown, discoverer of the newly reclassified "plutoid" object named Eris, which lies beyond Pluto in our solar system. "Water is what lubricates plate tectonics, which is what leads to the extreme difference between continents and seafloors, the large amount of earthquakes and volcanoes, fresh mountain-building. Venus has no water, no plate tectonics, no deep sea floor, no steep mountains, no continents, probably few earthquakes or volcanoes. A much less geologically interesting place!" "I doubt that in our galaxy typical stars have planets just like Earth around them," (University of Washington astronomer Don) Brownlee (author of the book "Rare Earth") said. "I'm sure there are lots of planets in the galaxy that are somewhat similar to Earth, but the idea that this is a typical planet is nonsensical."[93]

And a fourth article, a review of *Human*, a new book by Michael Gazzaniga, brings it down to our level:

Why do religious fundamentalists oppose the theory of evolution, despite the weight of evidence supporting it? The answer may lie with a deep-seated intuition that humans are qualitatively different from other

---

[92] *ScienceDaily* Aug. 8, 2008, www.sciencedaily.com/releases/2008/08/080807144236.htm
[93] Space.com, **What Makes Earth Special Compared to Other Planets,** Clara Moskowitz, 8 July 2008 www.space.com/scienceastronomy/080708-st-special-earth.html

animals—a difference so great that, for some, descent from a common ancestor is harder to imagine than the alternative.

As director of the University of California's SAGE Center for the Study of Mind in Santa Barbara, Michael Gazzaniga is no creationist. His confidence in our biological ties with the great apes is resolute. Yet, unlike many of his peers, Gazzaniga is not shy about trumpeting our special status in the animal kingdom. "We are a big deal and we are a little scared about it," he writes.... *Human*... explores recent research that shows that human brain structure, from gross anatomy down to the molecular scale, is significantly different from that of other species. Structural differences, in turn, reflect different cognitive functions, Gazzaniga says, often related to the demands of interacting with larger and more complex social groups.

These differences have led to our ability to construct alternate realities which can be played out as simulations in the mind's eye. This is a useful cognitive tool for forward planning, and it may also underlie the uniquely human impulses to create art and engage in scientific inquiry.[94]

What ought to become apparent from those articles is that science is always in flux, always looking at new evidence (or at old evidence in a new way) to come up with new ideas and concepts about how the universe is put together. As we wrote about earlier, this has been true for evolutionary theory for years; Stephen Jay Gould challenged the concept of gradualism as a part of the theory and forced the community to acknowledge that it was a significant problem, one that they have not yet dealt with in a way satisfactory to many. Other challenges loom for evolution, which we referred to earlier, even including challenges to random genetic mutations and natural selection as the operative forces in evolutionary history. What one reads in the press is clearly slanted in the direction of the standard model, but change will come, as it always does.

In what is perhaps the most important problem in all of science, the two finest scientific theories known to man, Relativity and Quantum Mechanics, are fundamentally incompatible. They don't work together. They are in conflict. The two theories that have given us every stitch of knowledge we have about the way the universe is constructed, from the largest (via the General Theory) to the smallest (via QM) cannot be reconciled.

---

[94] Review: *Human*, by Michael Gazzaniga, New Scientist Print Edition, by Ivan Semeniuk, 13 August 2008, www.newscientist.com/channel/opinion/mg19926692.100-review-ihumani-by-michael-gazzaniga.html

Knowing that, does it seem a bit silly to be stressed out about science and religion being incompatible at the moment, if in fact they are? And doesn't it seem a bit arrogant and immature to deny the existence of God on the basis of what will clearly be transient science? Further, for us as believers to try to reconcile that transient science with our own inadequate understanding of the creation story seems like a lot of wasted effort and energy, though it does sell books and pack conferences.

Recall that science once thought that the universe was infinitely old and large, something that flew straight in the face of Biblical creation. Then a bit of new science was theorized and then validated as evidence was discovered, and lo and behold, the universe had a starting point, along with space and time, and science and religion are reconciled, though you wouldn't know it by listening to the arguments about it. There are other points of reconciliation looming that nobody is really noticing, like the Mitochondrial Eve story that emerged in the 1980s.

Without going into the details, scientists discovered that all women were descended from one woman who lived in North Africa something like 100,000 to 250,000 years ago. The scientists themselves named her Mitochondrial Eve, the first word because the research was done via mitochondrial DNA. Not too long afterward, scientists discovered that all men seem to be descended from a small group of men who lived in North Africa about 100,000 to 250,000 years ago. I don't remember if they called them "Adam."

The actual dates have not quite been nailed down yet, the scientists quickly found an explanation that got them out from under the Garden of Eden story (it was a "genetic bottleneck"), and nobody noticed from within the faith that we now had an interesting dovetailing between science and religion. The discoveries did entirely reorient the field of anthropology, and now, rather than being heretical and sounding entirely too much like religion, the standard model has become (after much screaming and posturing) that humanity itself emerged from Africa after having appeared there as a species uniquely.

How did they get there? We have no answer for that yet in science, which is really irritating. Francis Crick and others note that the appearance of life itself is so unlikely that it must have come from somewhere off the planet entirely, whether planted by aliens from another civilization (and where did life originate in that civilization?) or from meteors, asteroids, and/or comets that somehow had the seeds of life buried within them. Science has almost fully moved away from life appearing on earth by random chance: it's just not possible. And so they look for other origins that are hardly less likely, but at least have not been ruled out by the math and physics yet.

So can we say that God just did it? He waved his magic wand and Adam and Eve just bounded onto the scene? That's what Genesis says. Could it be true?

You'll probably never read this anywhere else (I haven't), but the Boltzman Brain hypothesis gives us a quantum solution: humans did indeed just bound onto the scene, spontaneously produced by the energetic virtual vacuum of space. Zip! There they were. Nobody believes that, but the quantum does strange things. It's possible. We'll never know.

Since science is not yet reconciled even with itself, can we demand at any point in human history that religion and science be reconciled? Science and faith both liked the Flat Earth quite a bit, and the Geocentric and Heliocentric universes, and everyone seems to agree that Elvis and Bigfoot are living in Area 51. We will have periods of time when the science of that time will seem to mediate against the existence of God (as in the mechanistic, deterministic, reductionistic infinite universe) and other times when science will allow space for God to exist (the relativistic, quantum, chaotic and complex God). We'll never have proof, and the evidence will shift its weight around. People will use science to deny God, even if the science is strongly in favor. People will deny science to favor God, even if science is strongly against, or use science in bad and inappropriate, inaccurate ways both to deny and accept God. People will twist science to make it fit, for or against. The little 12-year-old Chloes of the world, of all ages and levels of intelligence, will cheerfully ignore whatever they need to ignore to believe whatever they want to believe.

And if there is no God, it doesn't matter either way. It's all delusion anyway.

But if God does exist, then it matters, because everything else is a delusion and there is only one reality, even if it's not what we think it is.

So is there anything in nature anywhere that we can always point to in order to be able to say, there is the evidence for God, as it says in Romans, that

> what may be known about God is plain to them, because God has made it plain to them. For since the creation of the world God's invisible qualities—his eternal power and divine nature—have been clearly seen, being understood from what has been made, so that men are without excuse. For although they knew God, they neither glorified him as God nor gave thanks to him, but their thinking became futile and their foolish hearts were darkened. Although they claimed to be wise, they became fools and exchanged the glory of the immortal God for images made to look like mortal man and birds and animals and reptiles.[95]

---

[95] Romans 1: 19-23 (NIV)

God's handiwork is there for Chloe to see, and there to deny, and science tells now to worship nature itself as a replacement for God and religion. It's an old book, Romans, but once again we are exchanging the glory of God to worship created things.

The evidence is there, revealed in nature. So what is it? "His eternal power and divine nature" are not phrases that reveal their meaning to us very easily. So let's take some guesses.

- *Eternal.* Outside of time and space, not contained or trapped by time and space, but above and beyond, somewhere else. We talked about this.
- *Power.* The power to create a universe out of nothing at all in an unimaginably tiny fraction of time, and the power to create that universe so that it would be ordered and would produce order, the power to give life to a universe via a few simple rules and interactions, just particles and forces and a compulsion to go from order to chaos and back again. Order. Order. Order.
- *Divine.* He is God. We are not. The universe is not. The creation is not. Created things are not. The particles and forces are not. The galaxies, the stars, the planets, earth itself are not. Life is not. Nature is not. Science is not. God is God. We are not.
- *Nature.* The character of God, revealed through nature, or if you want to play word games, his nature via his nature, *who* he is via *what* he created. The artist and his palette, his clay, his canvas, his handiwork revealed on a 93-billion light-year wide and deep, 13.7-billion-year-old piece of parchment, a scroll that when read will tell us something of who he is.

What is his nature? To paraphrase and complete Carl Sagan when he said that "the Cosmos is all that is, or ever was, or ever will be," in all that is, that was, and that ever will be, God's nature is revealed. The cosmos is a relational place, and thus God is a relational God. All of the order that he has imposed upon the cosmos is relational order, so obviously so that it almost becomes a tautology, so apparent that it almost seems foolish to notice it. He is an ordering God as creator, and in that order, he imposed relationship on the universe from its primal moments. If QM gives us a clue as to the origin of the universe, it took an observation by God to bounce the universe into being, an observation that is defined and apparent by looking at the quantum even now as it is aware of us as we interact with it. God interacted with Singularity in an almost casual and yet, according to quantum realities, deeply intimate way. And so we have a universe.

And as it headed along its merry way, its order manifested its power from the earliest moments as the forces emerged, and particles, and the particles interacted according to the forces, and began to clump. We need a more romantic and evocative word for "clumping," but the words we might use are a bit anthropomorphic—clumping into friendships, into families, into couples, into villages and towns and cities, into tribes and species and languages and cultures, clumping into commonalities and similarities. Even within science, we look for clumps of similarities; it is how we do science, looking for the sameness and the differences, and so we classify and analyze and organize. We mimic nature. We mimic God. The universe clumps. Nature clumps. We describe, and yet we miss the nature of God. We are the Clumpees. He is the Clumper. I'm betting that's the first time God and we have been described like that. We are clumps of space-time, clumps of stardust, clumps of particles and interactions. God (you read it here first) is not a clump.

Nothing lives well in isolation; in fact, nothing exists in isolation. Even quarks combine into threes—they are never alone. We exist only in relationship to the universe, to nature, to the forces and interactions and particles, and in relationship to the earth and to all that is on it and within it. We live in relationship to gravity, the strong force, the weak force, the electromagnetic force, bound together so intimately that we do not even know it. We live in relationship to the universe, to galaxies that give us order, to solar systems that give us structure and sustenance and protection, to the sun for its light and energy and gravity, to the planets that shield and awe us, to the earth itself that binds us in profound relationship. We live in relationship to the chemistry and the biology, to the chemicals that give us life, to water, to air, to energy, to the laws that transform them all into our life-support system.

We live in relationship to all of nature, dependent upon it for food and the things we think we need for a sustainable life. We are enmeshed in relationship with water and air and energy. We need plants and animals. We need weather and seasons. We need tectonic plates and carbon recycling. We need science and scientists. We need each other. We are more than the sum of our parts, more together than we are alone, more in community than in isolation, more, vastly more as the kingdom of believers than we ever could be as single people spending time alone with God.

We need each other. We need parents and relatives and friends. We need community, social structure, rules and regulations for living with each other. We need to be liked, to belong, to be loved, to be valued. We need a reason to live, a purpose, a meaning to life.

This is the character of God. This is his nature. He has created a universe that is relational, and the essence of relationship is a mutual co-dependency and free will. Call it yin and yang if you want, a balance, a symmetry, the Way, whether it be Tao or Jesus, and that is not to elevate all faiths to the level of Christianity, but to say that all faiths express the same longing and ask the same questions and offer some of the same answers: Why are we here? What is our meaning and purpose? Why do we suffer?

The universe is a symmetric sort of relational place; every particle its antiparticle, every force its particle, every action its equal and opposite reaction, every good deed creating a imbalance that impels another, every evil act creating a similar imbalance that is only corrected by forgiveness, grace, mercy, every evil act the result of other evil acts, every life with its own death, every true love with its true lover.

Ultimately it is all about the kingdom, because that is the ultimate relationship —God with his people. We broke our relationship with God and we create an imbalance in the fabric of the cosmos, an asymmetry, as we try to create the ultimate relationship with anything and everything except God, with any or all of the created things. Pick your moment in human history to find the god of that moment: we look with pity on primitive man as he worships fire, water, sun, moon, stars, volcanoes, or whatever, and we look with fear as modern man worships wealth, toys and possessions, sex, drugs, rock & roll, power and influence, position and status, nations and nation-states, freedom, individualism, democracy, capitalism, communism, socialism, tolerance and open-mindedness, and we see the scientists encourage us to worship again the stars and the galaxies, the wonders of nature, the power of the human mind. And it has all come full circle, our mighty minds and superior intellects taking us back to our original primitive state, worshipping still the created things rather than the creator.

Sagan, in that same speech, gives his thought on finding meaning, saying,

> The idea that our planet is at the center of the universe, much less that human purpose is central to the existence of the universe, is pathetic. Does life thereby lose all meaning? I think not. I think we make our lives meaningful by the courage of our questions, by the depth of our answers, by how widespread our understanding is of the essential tools for managing our future, for how skeptical we are of those in authority and of our obligation to care for one another.[96]

It's all very sweet, but completely delusional. If the real message of Genesis 1 is that God is God and that he and he alone is to be worshipped, that he is the creator of the created things and he alone is worthy, then it is easy to see where we have gone wrong and why the creation itself causes us so much pain and gives us so much pleasure. It is the nature of relationship that when betrayed, there is pain.

---

[96] SETI Carl Sagan Speech from 1995, http://seti.sentry.net/archive/public/1999/5-99/00000351.htm

On this point, we find common ground between believers and nonbelievers: we have violated our relationship with the planet, and there is pain. We will disagree somewhat on the nature of that violation; believers might accuse nonbelievers of having loved it too much and God too little, and nonbelievers will accuse believers of loving it not at all and abusing it to satisfy our own whims and desires. So let's find a different direction. Indeed, nonbelievers are in fact nonbelievers in God, and thus no matter what they have replaced God with, it is not God, and it is a violation of our relationship with God.

But for believers, we in fact have also replaced our love of God with a love for created things; in America, it is a love of comfort, wealth and prosperity, an idolatrous desire to be "blessed" with material things by a God whose primary role is to bless us with material things, with health and wealth and success. In truth, we have reduced God to being all about us, all about me, really, from my personal salvation to my personal God to my personal savior to my personal walk of faith to my personal call.

It's not about you. It's not about me. It's about God and it's about the kingdom.

Chapter 15

The Meaning of Life

There are, it seems, two places in our lives where some of us are granted the gift of intellectual, spiritual, existential crisis. The first we have discussed—suffering and the problem of Job. The second is meaning and how to find it. We have seen that there is no meaning possible without the existence of God, and then only if he decides to give it to us. It is always possible that even with a creator, there is no meaning to life, that there is no reason for any of us to be here.

The book of Job is all about suffering, and the answers were not altogether satisfying. There is another book that is all about meaning, about that intellectual, spiritual, existential crisis, and the answers are not altogether satisfying. It starts like this: "Meaningless! Meaningless!" says the Teacher. "Utterly meaningless! Everything is meaningless."[97] As we might have started reading Job and expected answers that would fit our preconceptions, so we might start reading Ecclesiastes by Solomon, son of David, and expect the answers to be uplifting and exalted, that we will find our meaning and purpose in serving God, fully realized as people.

So perhaps you want to be remembered, to make your mark on the planet. "There is no remembrance of men of old, and even those who are yet to come will not be remembered by those who follow."[98]

Or maybe you want to be smart, to do as our science friends suggest and have a life of learning. "For with much wisdom comes much sorrow; the more knowledge, the more grief."[99]

Pleasure? "I thought in my heart, 'Come now, I will test you with pleasure to find out what is good.' But that also proved to be meaningless. 'Laughter,' I said, 'is foolish. And what does pleasure accomplish?'"[100]

Hard work?

> I denied myself nothing my eyes desired; I refused my heart no pleasure. My heart took delight in all my work, and this was the reward for all my labor. Yet when I surveyed all that my hands had done and

---

[97] Ecclesiastes 1: 2 (NIV)
[98] Ecclesiastes 1: 11 (NIV)
[99] Ecclesiastes 1: 18 (NIV)
[100] Ecclesiastes 2: 1, 2 (NIV)

what I had toiled to achieve, everything was meaningless, a chasing after the wind; nothing was gained under the sun."[101]

Will you pursue wisdom?

> I saw that wisdom is better than folly, just as light is better than darkness. The wise man has eyes in his head, while the fool walks in the darkness; but I came to realize that the same fate overtakes them both. Then I thought in my heart, "The fate of the fool will overtake me also. What then do I gain by being wise?" I said in my heart, "This too is meaningless." For the wise man, like the fool, will not be long remembered; in days to come both will be forgotten. Like the fool, the wise man too must die![102]

Perhaps wealth is the way:

> Whoever loves money never has money enough; whoever loves wealth is never satisfied with his income. This too is meaningless. As goods increase, so do those who consume them. And what benefit are they to the owner except to feast his eyes on them? The sleep of a laborer is sweet, whether he eats little or much, but the abundance of a rich man permits him no sleep. I have seen a grievous evil under the sun: wealth hoarded to the harm of its owner, or wealth lost through some misfortune, so that when he has a son there is nothing left for him. Naked a man comes from his mother's womb, and as he comes, so he departs. He takes nothing from his labor that he can carry in his hand.[103]

> So I hated life, because the work that is done under the sun was grievous to me. All of it is meaningless, a chasing after the wind.[104]

> I have seen the burden God has laid on men. He has made everything beautiful in its time. He has also set eternity in the hearts of men; yet they cannot fathom what God has done from beginning to end. I know that there is nothing better for men than to be happy and do good while they live. That everyone may eat and drink, and find satisfaction in all his toil—this is the gift of God. I know that everything God does

---

[101] Ecclesiastes 2: 10, 11 (NIV)
[102] Ecclesiastes 2: 13-16 (NIV)
[103] Ecclesiastes 5: 10-15 (NIV)
[104] Ecclesiastes 2: 17 (NIV)

will endure forever; nothing can be added to it and nothing taken from it. God does it so that men will revere him.[105]

And finally, after much more meaninglessness and existential angst and despair, Solomon concludes,

> Remember your Creator in the days of your youth, before the days of trouble come and the years approach when you will say, "I find no pleasure in them." Remember him—before...the dust returns to the ground it came from, and the spirit returns to God who gave it.
>
> "Meaningless! Meaningless!" says the Teacher. "Everything is meaningless!"
>
> Now all has been heard; here is the conclusion of the matter: Fear God and keep his commandments, for this is the whole duty of man. For God will bring every deed into judgment, including every hidden thing, whether it is good or evil.[106]

This is not the happy place to find ourselves. Here's the conclusion: nothing in life has any meaning without God, and that meaning is defined around God and his interaction with us, on his terms, and those alone.

Sagan actually does a mostly fine job of summing up the meaninglessness of our normative human existence in his speech when he describes how pathetic our seemingly vast human pursuits are:

> I look at that dot [earth from a distance of several billion miles away in space, caught in a sunbeam] and I think that's here, that's home, that's us. On that dot everyone you love, everyone you know, everyone you ever heard of, every humanbeing who ever lived, lived out their lives. The aggregate of all our joy and suffering, thousands of confident and mutually exclusive religions, ideologies and economic doctrines, every hunter and forager, every hero and coward, every creator and destroyer of civilization, every king and peasant, every young couple in love, every mother and father, every hopeful child, every inventor and explorer, every revered teacher of morals, every corrupt politician, every superstar, every supreme leader, every saint and sinner in the

---

[105] Ecclesiastes 3: 10-14 (NIV)
[106] Ecclesiastes 12: 1, 7, 8, 13, 14 (NIV)

history of our species lived there on a mote of dust suspended in a sunbeam.

The earth is a very small stage in a vast cosmic arena. Think of the rivers of blood spilled by all those generals and emperors so that in glory and triumph they could become the momentary masters of a fraction of a dot. Think of the endless cruelties visited by the inhabitants of one corner of the dot on the scarcely distinguishable inhabitants of some other corner of the dot. How frequent their misunderstandings, how eager they are to kill one another, how fervent their hatreds. Think of those who derived their self-esteem from dividing the dot into two hundred still littler patches.

Our posturings, our imagined self-importance, the delusion that we  have some privileged position in the universe are challenged by this point of pale light. Our planet is a lonely speck in a great enveloping cosmic dark. In our obscurity, in all this vastness there is no hint that help will come from elsewhere to save us from ourselves; it is up to us.

It's been said that astronomy is a humbling and even character building experience. There is perhaps no better demonstration of the folly of human conceits than this distant image of our tiny world. For me, it underscores our responsibility, our profound responsibility to deal more kindly with one another and to preserve and cherish that pale blue dot; the only home we have ever known.[107]

His critique of us humans is apt and appropriate—we have a vastly inflated opinion of ourselves as a planet and a species. Without God, we have no value. On our own, we have no value. We pathetically fight over doctrines and beliefs and territories. And we must be honest—we who have faith in God do it, too, participating in and even instigating many of the horrors humanity has inflicted upon itself. We people of faith, acting in fear that God needs us to defend him,

---

[107] SETI Carl Sagan Speech from 1995, http://seti.sentry.net/archive/public/1999/5-99/00000351.htm

148

do and have done terrible things, eager to kill one another, fervently hating, committed to a small patch of land on that pale blue dot floating in a sea of nothingness.

But where in a reductionist universe, our "privileged position" might be "challenged by this point of pale light," in God's universe, where the tiny and insignificant become the repositories of meaning, the size of the dot is irrelevant and humanity's value is not defined and determined by the size and insignificance of that dot. Our value is defined and determined by God, imparted by God, created by God, intended by God, and only by God. There is no other path to follow, no other direction to go, no other meaning to pursue than this.

It is not just in astronomy that we are humbled and our characters built, not just there that our human conceits are exposed as folly. In God's universe, we have indeed a "profound responsibility to deal more kindly with one another and to preserve and cherish that pale blue dot," but not because Carl tells us that it is true. It is not because if we do not do so, we will not survive as a species, because in Carl's universe, we will not survive as a species, even if we do not manage to make ourselves extinct. The universe will eventually take care of that for us, as it moves ponderously and inexorably toward maximum entropy with no structure, no possibility of life, no option for order. For Carl, it is about survival, and that is the only thing that has value, because that is the way his universe is put together.

God's universe is different. We have a "profound responsibility to deal more kindly with one another and to preserve and cherish that pale blue dot" because those are his commandments, and the meaning we will find in life is in fearing God and following his commandments. We are to love God and love each other, not so that we will survive, but because it is in the richness of those interactions and relationships that life will gain its power and joy and beauty. Existence in God's universe is not just about survival; maybe it's not even about survival at all. After all, "Greater love has no one than this, that he lay down his life for his friends."[108]

God's universe is about relationships, and the highest form of relationship is love. That, finally, is the ultimate goal and purpose of the universe, to produce and sustain creatures capable of love, love with each other, love with and for God, and for God to love in return. The purpose of the universe is summed up in three words, one small throwaway sentence that anyone of any level of intelligence can understand and apply—God is love. "Whoever does not love does not know God, because God is love."[109]

---

[108] John 15:13 (NIV)

[109] 1 John 4:8 (NIV)

In fact, we need to see this entire passage, because it is the totality:

> Let us love one another, for love comes from God. Everyone who loves has been born of God and knows God. Whoever does not love does not know God, because God is love. This is how God showed his love among us: He sent his one and only Son into the world that we might live through him. This is love: not that we loved God, but that he loved us and sent his Son as an atoning sacrifice for our sins. Dear friends, since God so loved us, we also ought to love one another. No one has ever seen God; but if we love one another, God lives in us and his love is made complete in us. We know that we live in him and he in us, because he has given us of his Spirit. And we have seen and testify that the Father has sent his Son to be the Savior of the world. If anyone acknowledges that Jesus is the Son of God, God lives in him and he in God. And so we know and rely on the love God has for us. God is love. Whoever lives in love lives in God, and God in him. In this way, love is made complete among us so that we will have confidence on the day of judgment, because in this world we are like him. There is no fear in love. But perfect love drives out fear, because fear has to do with punishment. The one who fears is not made perfect in love. We love because he first loved us. If anyone says, "I love God," yet hates his brother, he is a liar. For anyone who does not love his brother, whom he has seen, cannot love God, whom he has not seen. And he has given us this command: Whoever loves God must also love his brother.[110]

Poor old Carl, and poor old Solomon. Solomon could find no more meaning than fearing God and following his commands, terrified of the punishment to come. Carl has a deep sense of how profoundly we need to cherish each other and the planet, but he is little better than Solomon—it's all about survival.

And poor old many-of-us, because we still live in fear of punishment, and in fear that we will lose our comforts and freedoms to others who might threaten us, and so we act in fear, hatred, revenge, and retribution, trying to force balance into an unbalanced world by virtue of wars, oppression, unjust laws, and many of the things that Carl so justly accused us of.

But the meaning of life is found so easily—love God, love each other. In love there is no room for fear, for selfishness, for rivers of blood, for endless cruelties, for misunderstandings, for eagerness to kill, for fervent hatreds, for getting our self-esteem by virtue of the countries we live in, as Carl accuses us of doing, nor for finding our meaning in science, in reason, in religion or

---

[110] 1 John 4:7-21 (NIV)

comforts or freedoms, nor in any of the things where we might seek to find a meaning and purpose in life. All is delusion, all is meaningless, everything is folly outside of the love of God for us, and us for God, and because there is no reason to do otherwise, in our love for each other in spite of our selfishness and conceits.

And so, the fractal Jesus.

> This is how God showed his love among us: He sent his one and only Son into the world that we might live through him. This is love: not that we loved God, but that he loved us and sent his Son as an atoning sacrifice for our sins. Dear friends, since God so loved us, we also ought to love one another.[111]

Here is the real miracle, as we have said: it is not that God does not love us enough to heal us of all our diseases or protect us from the evils of the world. It is not that God does not love us enough. It is that he loves us at all.

And his love for us is not expressed in daily protections like clearing up pimples or finding parking spots, nor is it expressed in healing cancers or keeping storms at bay. It was and is expressed in showing us his character through Jesus, and that character is not just to create order and allow relationships to emerge through the workings of nature. That character is love for us, the center of meaning in his creation, as astronomer Alan Dressler terms it, created in his image as observers, capable of fully realized relationships of deep and profound love for him and each other, not a love just as a mother for her helpless infant, though there are those moments, but a love that grows and matures, that understands the width and depth and height of love that cannot be separated, lover from beloved, by anything, not by pain, suffering, tragedy, hardship, betrayal, infidelity, not by the winds of fate or the vagaries of time and space, not by hatreds or fears or selfish conceits.

It is the nature of love that it is sacrificial, as mother and father for infant and toddler, as husband for wife and wife for husband, as soldier for country, as martyr for God, as God for mankind and man for God. The ultimate in sacrifice is giving one's life for another. We know this to be true.

And so, the fractal Jesus, God as man showing us the character of God and demonstrating his love for us through the ultimate sacrifice, an unimpeded sacrifice of life for the lives and eternities of others, to do what needed to be done to establish the basis as love for building the kingdom. It is not a kingdom based on commands or rules, regulations, the laws of man or nature or even

---

[111] 1 John 4:9-11 (NIV)

God, but a kingdom based on love. How would we know that God loved us if we had not seen it, and if we had not been responsible for his death ourselves? How much more could it have been expressed than as forgiveness, mercy and grace for what we did and do to deny our love for God, to be our own people in charge of our own fates? We tried to make the son of God pathetic, and by that, God himself, and to exalt ourselves to the Godhead, the created masquerading as the creator, man as god, as pathetic a sight in Carl's universe as one could imagine.

And so, the fractal Jesus, "the image of the invisible God, the firstborn over all creation,"[112] and the fractal Us, "We love because he first loved us. If anyone says, "I love God," yet hates his brother, he is a liar. For anyone who does not love his brother, whom he has seen, cannot love God, whom he has not seen. And he has given us this command: Whoever loves God must also love his brother."[113]

Love is a fractal. It is infinite, each piece a reflection, an image of the whole, and yet whole in and of itself, each point of love an infinity of love. And love is the image of God. We are not God, but we can be like God, each one of us a point, a pale blue dot of love in a grand infinity of love, no point alone, every point significant, but only really as a part of the whole. Each tiny fractalated bit of love is distinct and unique, each relationship of love possessed of its own flavor of richness and beauty, but just like all of the infinity of points of love that curl up inside the eternal depths of the simple fractal of love.

Stretching the point? Well, of course. That's what a fractal is.

Complexity Theory comes out of Chaos Theory, often called "The Edge of Chaos". It finds the place where a tiny, insignificant point explodes out of itself to become a universe of points, and in fact, every point in a fractal has the potential to be that cosmos of points, and out of that potential, every point indeed is a universe of points if you look closely enough.

And so each one of us has the God-created, God-inspired potential to have a universe of impact on the Kingdom. Evidence that God has always and will always use the tiny and insignificant for extraordinarily significant things? As above, Jesus, of course, but not only Jesus. The Bible in its entirety is a story of God finding, inspiring and enabling impossibly tiny and insignificant people in ways that wrote the story itself. Adam, Eve, Noah, Abraham, Lot, Hagar, Ishmael, Sarah, Isaac, Rebekah, Jacob/Israel the deceiver, Rachel, Joseph the

---

[112] Colossians 1:15 (NIV)
[113] 1 John 4:7-21 (NIV)

arrogant, Moses the murderer, Aaron, Joshua, Rahab the prostitute, Samson the fool, Ruth, Naomi, Samuel the child, Saul the weak, David the adulterer and murderer, Solomon who brought idols into Israel, Isaiah, Jeremiah, Ezekiel, Amos, Peter the satan and denier, Andrew, James, John, Judas Iscariot the betrayer, Matthew the tax collector, Saul the persecutor, and the list goes on and on. Tiny, insignificant bits of DNA lost in an indifferent universe, alive for less than a breath, pointless and meaningless, except that God's still, small voice called them gently and they listened and heard and obeyed and the fractal exploded into the story of the Messiah.

None of them perfect, none of us perfect, none of us God, but all of us with a Singular potential, all of us a point of the fractal Jesus, any of us able to do more than imaginable, God using tiny, insignificant points to create a universe from each, the kingdom of God emerging from the interaction and relationships between the points. None of us are the kingdom, but the kingdom emerges from all of us, together.

Chapter 16

Lucy, You Got Some 'Splainin' to Do

With apologies to Dezi Arnez and Lucille Ball, we got some 'splainin' to do. Like, where are we and what does any of this mean?

Let's start with a piece of an interview with Susan Jacoby, atheist, former reporter for the *Washington Post* and program director of the Center for Inquiry-New York City (the sponsor of Camp Inquiry earlier). She is the author of five books, including *Wild Justice*, a Pulitzer Prize finalist, and *Freethinkers: A History of American Secularism*. Her political blog, The Secularist's Corner, is on the Web site of the *Washington Post*.

> I'm one of the village atheists on *Faith,* a panel sponsored by the *Washington Post* and *Newsweek*. In a recent post I wrote that when I was 7 years old, I was taken by my mom to visit a friend who had been stricken by polio and was in an iron lung. Polio has basically been eradicated, but I grew up when polio was still a real threat to children, before the Salk vaccine.
>
> This childhood friend had been playing and running only three weeks before, and now he was in an iron lung. And I asked my mom, "Why would God let something like that happen?" And to her credit, instead of giving me some moronic answer, my mother said, "I don't know."[114]

And to Ms. Jacoby's credit, she doesn't say that she became an atheist on the spot at age 7, but it did start a long process that culminated in her abandoning any grip she may have had on faith and becoming a leader in what one might call the cult of rationalism. Her question as a child stands for all of us regardless of age: why would God let something like that happen?

The answers offered to us by Job and Solomon are the truth, but they are harsh and unsatisfying. They will continue to be the final answers, but there may be other answers along the way that will help. Whether any of them will satisfy is hard to say.

---

[114] **How Anti-Intellectualism Is Destroying America**, by Terrence McNally, AlterNet., August 15, 2008., www.alternet.org/story/95109/

An article in *Harper's* magazine [115] gives an interesting thought and perspective: one day, at the start of a new year, nobody dies, and the question arises, what if nobody continues to die, if everyone continues to live forever? The article briefly explores the issue of the church, implying that the church exists only because of death, our fear of it, and our need to defeat it in the afterlife, but the question is far larger than just death. It is, in fact, life.

There are levels to our struggle with suffering, and death is at the core, so one needs to start with death. From a purely scientific perspective, in looking at the planet and thinking of sustainability, death is part and parcel of the package. We don't have to spend much time talking about the cycles of life and death that surround us, about the need for some things to die in order for others to live, except to say that ultimately, everything must die in order for everything else to be able to continue to live.

If nothing died, if somehow we didn't need to eat in order to survive so that nothing was ever killed for food, not a peach or a pear, not an ear of corn or a potato, not a cow, a pig, or a chicken, and if everything continued to live without dying, then long ago we would have all ceased to have a real existence, sort of like parents with children or Jennifer without Brad. We would have crowded each other off the land into the water, the water would have filled with life until there was no room for either water or living things, and in the absence of death altogether, we would be lying in sweating mile-high stinking mounds of foul flesh, and if not now, then eventually. There is no room on the planet for life to exist without death.

Death is a part of the construct of the universe. Antiparticles and particles arrive and annihilate each other. Gas clouds collapse into stars, stars are born, persist, and explode or fizzle out, galaxies devour each other, black holes eat other black holes and stars and perhaps even galaxies. The universe itself is on a path to non-existence, whether through heat death, the Big Rip (when Dark Energy rips everything apart down to the proton level), or the Big Crunch, the (now highly unlikely) recollapse into Singularity, or the Big Chill, in which things just gradually lose their heat. Space-time itself has no guarantee of persisting. There is no real state of stasis in the universe. Change is part of the process, and the last part of change is death in one form or another.

Death is a normative part of human existence and always has been, as far as science is concerned, and interestingly enough, while criticizing people of faith for using their religion as a crutch to vanquish death, scientists are now deeply enmeshed in attempts to extend life far beyond its current length off into what they hope will be forever. In this paradigm, death can be defeated by science and we will live forever, although we will apparently be saved from mile-high

---

[115] **A new paradise or a new hell**, Jose Saramago, from his novel *Death with Interruptions*, in Harper's Magazine, Sept 2008, pp 29-30

pulsating mounds of stinking flesh by the fact that extended life will only be for those very few who can afford it. It is the new religion, very much like our old religions, terrified of death, of not existing, like Jared was terrified at Camp Inquiry earlier, science trying to find a loophole that is more than just throwing water balloons at the problem.

So perhaps the question is not really about death, but about our fear of death. Death is normal. Always has been. Why can't we just get used to it? Why don't we just accept it and move on, at least until we have moved on? Surely in a rational, reasonable, reductionist universe, we should long ago have learned to accept death with hardly a backwards glance, nothing more inevitably representative of the way nature works than death, and nothing more useful, really. Death allows those who remain to have sufficient resources to continue to live —enough food, air, water, space, and the perks of life on a rich and vibrant planet. You had your time. Go away now. It's my time.

But humans don't do that, never have, never will. Death remains terrifying in its inevitability and relentlessness. Death is the great leveler; no matter how bright the Brights are, they die just like ignorant, savage primitive religious people, and as much knowledge as they have, they have no more knowledge than the stupidest among us about what comes after. They will tell us, somehow smug and self-satisfied, that nothing comes after, that death is the end, but they have no evidence except the lack of evidence that anything actually does happen after death.

Before they jump all over me here, let me just remind them of how fond they are of the multiverse, that concept they use to tell us that our universe is not Finely Tuned for humans because this universe is just one of many, though of course they have no evidence of any other universe than this one. That sword cuts both ways. We all want comfort. Religion provides comfort. The multiverse provides comfort. There is more evidence for the former.

We might then suggest, from an evolutionary perspective, that our own survival is of paramount importance to us, and the fear we have of dying is bred within us over millennia of trying to survive.

Why then are we upset when family and friends die? Well, it must be because we want our collective gene pool to survive, again bred within us over vast reaches of time.

Then why would any of us ever ask the question, "Why would God let something like that happen?" when our friend is taken off the playground and the swing set to live the rest of his life in an iron lung? Where does that pain come from, the pain we feel when a son or a daughter suffers, or a wife or husband, a mother, a father, or even and maybe especially a pet dog or cat?

How can we as reasonable, rational scientific thinkers possibly justify the pain we feel when our old dog takes the injection so trustingly, looks up at us, shivers a bit, and collapses into death? Why does the sight of that tongue suddenly hanging limply out of the mouth drive a knife into our souls? What part of us is ripped out and torn asunder when policemen or soldiers walk slowly up to the front door and stand there, unable to speak, unable to give us the news that we know, suddenly, has thrust itself obscenely into our calm, ordered existence? Why do we desperately, horribly need an answer to the question that we scream into that night and many other nights, why have you let this happen to me? Why did you not love me and protect me from the unspeakable agony that gashes and gnaws at the core of my being and existence?

The first part of the answer is easy: it is because we love. It is because there is love in the universe. It is because the nature and character of God is love, we are the creatures that he loves, the creatures that love him back, and we do not understand why a God of love would let something like that happen. Why would a God of love create a universe with so much pain, so much suffering, so much struggle, so much cruelty?

Love is the cause. It is the reason, the source, the origin, the Big Bang of pain in life. Without love, there is no pain. If you have no love, you do not hurt, except when you hurt for yourself, and animals do that, so that's not so important, really, is it?

Of course, we have a word for people who do not love others, who only love themselves. We call them sociopaths, psychopaths, people without consciences, and we call them monsters. They live in history as hideous creatures of the night who crept out as Jack the Ripper, the Boston Strangler, the Hillside Rapist, the Zodiac Killer, cannibal Jeffrey Dahmer, Ted Bundy, John Wayne Gacy, Henry Lee Lucas, and so many more. For each, it was "survival of the fittest" that defined their existence, and for many of them, they were the fittest: Jack and the Zodiac were never caught, and the others only after dozens, hundreds, probably even thousands of killings (Lucas alone is thought to have murdered 3000, though we do not and may never know.)

Their opposites are those who sacrificed everything for others, including life itself. When Arland D. Williams Jr., a passenger on Air Florida Flight 90 that crashed into the Potomac, passed the rescue line once, twice, three times to others who were clinging to the wreckage in icy water, and then drowned before he himself could be rescued, nobody accused him of stupidity or sociopathy. He was and remains a hero, as are all those in war and peace who sacrifice themselves for others, the supreme act of love.

Love is the problem. Without it, we wouldn't care what happens to others. And yet, we do. Why do we care, and why does it bother us so much that God doesn't seem to? Though there are many things we don't understand, we understand love. But we don't understand God's love because it doesn't do what love is supposed to do. Love is supposed to protect, to do everything in its power to protect, and since God is omni-powerful, then he should omni-protect.

And clearly he does not.

And clearly, we want to know why not.

We can go around and around on this one, but let's just go to the finish line first, and then run the race. Here's the issue: God created a universe with free will and choice in it, and then rotated the entire thing around interactions/relationships and, ultimately, love. People have a choice to love God and love each other. I guess love has to be a choice; otherwise, it's compelled, acquired, in-bred, instinctive, or randomly generated via genetic mutation and natural selection.

So people have a real choice whether to act in a loving way or not, and are confronted with this choice on a moment-by-moment basis with hardly a break. People also have their own self-interest to consider, so we are all participating in this balancing act between love for God, love for others, and love for self, trying to figure out when to sacrifice what and how.

It's quite a challenge. It's a lot easier if you don't believe in God, but it's still not easy. The easiest is when you only love yourself, but then you become a sociopath. Not a good option, though probably the most pleasant, if also the most evil. If you find your way through that minefield, you'll end up as a dictator or a titan of industry. If not, you end up hiding bodies in the back yard.

And many of the evil deeds in history come from that tension; not the sociopathic tension, but the tension between loving God, loving others, and loving one's self. One might be tempted to suggest that we each have a sociopath and a hero lurking deep within us, each ready to emerge depending on the timing and orientation of the moment, and every human develops and has developed throughout history a certain skill in making choices seem rational, even and especially the sociopaths.

None of the people we might now call the monsters of history felt that they were doing anything monstrous: Hitler (we always have to start with him), Stalin, Mao, Pol Pot, Papa Doc, Baby Doc, Pinochet, Marcos, all of them felt that they were being heroic as national leaders. We could probably say the same about leaders who are on the winning sides and whose roles in history were written from an entirely different perspective, but many of the things that the winners did were no more honorable nor loving, even in our own country—you can read about those in that other book I wrote.

What is interesting, though, is that where we seem to have this faint revulsion and a feeling of pity, disgust, horror, and helplessness when it comes to the genocides and the slaughters that history feeds upon, we save our most powerful emotions for the tragedies that happen to, well, us. Thus, we become Job.

Why would that accusation be made? Job was most concerned about the things that concerned Job, that is, his own sufferings and losses. At no point did he talk about the suffering of others in far-off lands, even in a theoretical, "this must be happening" sort of way. Neither did his friends. They were all focused on Job, his troubles, and his alleged sins.

So I read about the little child who had to live in an iron lung up above, and I feel a brief moment of pity. If I myself were forced to do the same, I would be crying out to God for healing and cursing him when he did not listen, and if it happened to my friend and playmate, then I would want to know, as Ms. Jacoby did, why God would let that happen.

That's logical. Of course, I am more concerned with myself and my immediate circle of family and friends than I am about strangers across the planet. I can't be expected to care about them as much as I do about those whom I love.

But we each live in our own expanding circle of indifference. The further the tragedy gets away from me, the less I can be expected to care about it, unless the tragedy is world-class, such as those like Hurricane Katrina, the south Asian tsunami, the genocide in Darfur, and many others.

But even then, we are driven by what we are told matters—3000 people died on 9/11 in the Towers and the Pentagon, and that event continues to dominate US and world events, but 3000 people in the US dying of cancer every two days or 30,000 children globally dying every day of hunger and hunger-related diseases is old news. Perhaps it's not fair to point it out, but we are not pure in how we react to tragedy.

In fact, we react to tragedy according to the same framework that love is constructed under: God, others, and self. We condemn God, reject him, deny his existence because he does not prevent the tragedies that upset *us*. We aren't quite as upset over the tragedies that happen to others, and we never seem to wonder about the tragedies that upset God. When it comes to reacting to tragedies, we lean heavily toward being sociopaths, concerned mostly about ourselves, and less so about others in that expanding circle of indifference until there is a point where, because we are humans and limited in our scope and reach, we really don't care that much at all. It might be a distance in scope and size, in space and distance, or in time, but there is a place where we are pretty indifferent toward the most terrible things that have happened in all of human history.

Shall we think that God is indifferent to those because he seems indifferent to mine? Shall we presume to know the mind and heart of God? Do we really want to think that because we have no answer to the question, "Why would a God of love let something like that happen?" that there is no answer?

Because the answer is this: either he cares, or he does not. And do you really think that he does not?

So we are back to Job. God is the God of all. He cares for everything in his creation. He lists them, he numbers them, he goes on and on about his care, love, and concern for his creation.

As a part of that creation, he gives you and me and all of the humans who have ever lived free will.

As a part of that free will, we are his agents of love on the planet. He abrogates his role as observer to us, and he gives to us the role of lovers, lovers of God, lovers of each other, lovers of ourselves. On that basis, the potential for the greatest and the most monstrous acts of evil is created, and they are realized through us and our choices, along with the most profound and beautiful acts of good. We are the lovers, and we are the sociopaths, and we oscillate between the two extremes, and there is good and evil on the planet.

Now we have to go back to talk about death some more. If we as humans have to take responsibility for evil deeds, we cannot be held responsible for hurricanes, earthquakes, disease, famine, drought, floods, tornadoes, and all of the "acts of God" that cause so much death and suffering. They are "acts of God." They're his fault, a lousy, imperfect world, poorly designed, poorly executed, poorly maintained. As "Saul has slain his thousands, and David his tens of thousands,"[116] so we have slain our tens of millions, and God, through nature, his hundreds of millions, and through the act of having created a planet that includes death, God has slain all of us, all of the many billions who have ever lived, all of the billions who now live, and the untold billions who have yet to be conceived.

We may be responsible for our share of those deaths, but surely God has the greater responsibility, since it is his game, his design, his grand plan for which it somehow is necessary for death and suffering to play a major role. Further, the suffering is immense and unthinkable, indescribable in its horror, and it is not only humans who inflict the horrors on each other, but nature that inflicts its own indescribable horrors in ways that make Stephen King seem dullish and without skill or imagination in horrors.

---

[116] 1Samuel 18:7 (NIV)

Now I am Job, and I stand at God's portals and scream into his face that this is not right, not fair, not just. We are just idiots and cannot bear the responsibility we have been given to treat each other rightly. Anyone would have known not to give us the ability we have to hate each other along with the tools we have created to hurt each other. And even if we did not, the planet itself with its groanings and shudderings will slaughter us even as we try to live our lives, making innocent decisions to plan, for example, a December 2004 vacation in Banda Aceh or Sri Lanka or, forced by our need to survive, to build our houses in the flood plains of Bangladesh or in the shadows of Vesuvius, Krakatoa, or Mt. St. Helens.

I no longer am wondering, how could a loving God let my playmate end up in an iron lung, but how could a loving God create a planet and a people that would have to endure such horror, die such monstrous, pointless deaths, suffer such endless agonies, and leave the ultimate reason mysterious and unknowable?

God answers Job, as he answers all of us, and the answer must satisfy, because it is the only answer. He is God, and we are not.

We have then a choice to make. Either we get rid of God altogether because his answer to this question does not satisfy our tiny and insignificant sociopathic minds, or we realize that without a God, even the question itself has no meaning.

This again is not the happy place. What we have to admit is that we are trying to convict God on a charge that only has meaning if God exists, on terms of morality that only exist if God defines them, on accusations of horror and terror that are only horrible and terrible if God has created a universe where such things can be defined.

Richard Dawkins must be quoted again: The universe "has precisely the properties we should expect if there is, at bottom, no design, no purpose, no evil and no good, nothing but pointless indifference."[117] If God does not exist, then none of the things that we think are evil can in fact be described as evil. They are not evil. They just . . . are. They are just part of the pointlessness of a pointless universe, part of the meaninglessness of a meaningless cosmos. There is neither evil nor good. Nothing is evil. Not acts of God, since without God, there are no acts of God, not the actions of man, nothing that happens anywhere at any time for any natural reason, and the only reasons there are, are natural, and are neither good nor evil.

---

[117] Richard Dawkins, *The Selfish Gene*

So in order for me to scream at God, I have to condemn God on his terms. I have to acknowledge and admit that he exists and that he is the God who gets to define what is right and what is wrong.

And then I have the audacity to tell him that he is wrong. His answer is Job's answer, first from Elihu:

> So listen to me, you men of understanding. Far be it from God to do evil, from the Almighty to do wrong. . . . Men cry out under a load of oppression; they plead for relief from the arm of the powerful. But no one says, 'Where is God my Maker, who gives songs in the night, who teaches more to us than to the beasts of the earth and makes us wiser than the birds of the air?' He does not answer when men cry out because of the arrogance of the wicked. Indeed, God does not listen to their empty plea; the Almighty pays no attention to it. How much less, then, will he listen when you say that you do not see him, that your case is before him and you must wait for him, and further, that his anger never punishes and he does not take the least notice of wickedness. . . . How great is God—beyond our understanding! The number of his years is past finding out.[118]

And then God himself honors Job by speaking to him:

> The Lord said to Job: "Will the one who contends with the Almighty correct him? Let him who accuses God answer him!"
>
> Then Job answered the Lord: "I am unworthy—how can I reply to you? I put my hand over my mouth. I spoke once, but I have no answer—twice, but I will say no more."
>
> Then the Lord spoke to Job out of the storm: "Brace yourself like a man; I will question you, and you shall answer me. Would you discredit my justice? Would you condemn me to justify yourself? Do you have an arm like God's, and can your voice thunder like his? Then adorn yourself with glory and splendor, and clothe yourself in honor and majesty. Unleash the fury of your wrath, look at every proud man and bring him low, look at every proud man and humble him, crush the wicked where they stand. Bury them all in the dust together; shroud their faces in the grave. Then I myself will admit to you that your own

---

[118] Job 34: 10, 35: 9-15, 36: 26 (NIV)

right hand can save you... Who has a claim against me that I must pay? Everything under heaven belongs to me."[119]

Job's answer to God must then be ours:

> Then Job replied to the Lord : "I know that you can do all things; no plan of yours can be thwarted. You asked, 'Who is this that obscures my counsel without knowledge?' Surely I spoke of things I did not understand, things too wonderful for me to know."[120]

David speaks similarly:

> My heart is not proud, O Lord, my eyes are not haughty; I do not concern myself with great matters or things too wonderful for me. But I have stilled and quieted my soul; like a weaned child with its mother, like a weaned child is my soul within me. O Israel, put your hope in the Lord both now and forevermore.[121]

God is God, and we are not. Nothing he does is wrong, and we are reduced to accusing him on his own terms, since without him, there are no terms. He makes the rules, and if we don't like it, then we live in a delusional universe of no rules at all in clear violation of the obvious reality that there are rules. That's insane.

God is God, and we are not.

---

[119] Job 40: 1-14, 41: 11 (NIV)
[120] Job 42: 1-3 (NIV)
[121] Psalm 131: 1-3 (NIV)

Chapter 17
It's All God's Fault. OK, Not Really.

There are no guarantees. None of us know how long we will live or when or how we will die. Will we die in the womb, at birth, as an infant? Will we live long and die in our sleep? Will we die well or horribly, naturally or unnaturally? Will we drop dead on a golf course, or linger in a cancer ward?

Somehow when we rage at God over death and his unwillingness to heal or prevent disease or injury, we make an assumption that we would all deny making—that it really isn't fair unless we all live to a certain age and then die quietly in our sleep with our families gathered around us in loving adoration. We have built within us a certain age that you are supposed to reach, and if life-threatening disease or accident comes before that age, then we pray, fast, and beseech the Lord as David did for his own child. We expect, without knowing it, that we will not die before our time, that we will be healed of our diseases miraculously, because that is God's role to fulfill.

In another book, I told the story of telling an adult class at a church that it was not God's main job to keep us comfortable. There was a long pause, and then a voice from the back said with feeling, "Well, what *is* it then?" We have reduced our God to that which takes care of our needs. He's more of a maid or a slave than a God. It's his job to keep us healthy, wealthy, happy and wise.

Let's just think about how foolish that is. First, if God kept all Christians healthy, wealthy, happy and wise, then evangelism would be a no-brainer. Everybody else would be sick and dying and we would be living in mansions and eating bonbons all day long. They'd all want to become Christians, and either that would be for the *right* reason or the *wrong* reason, the reason being, I want to be Healthy, Wealthy, Happy and Wise, too. We'll call that HWHW, or, since I'm a math guy, $(HW)^2$.

That's the wrong reason, and if it's the wrong reason under that scenario, then it's the wrong reason all the time, including right now. We didn't become believers because of $(HW)^2$, so we shouldn't expect it to be a part of the package. And yet, we do. Suffering isn't supposed to happen to *me*. Or to the people I know and love. It's supposed to happen to *others*. God's supposed to protect me and mine. Unfortunately, me and mine are somebody else to somebody else who wants God to protect them and theirs. We all want God to protect us and ours at the expense of them and theirs.

Kinda puts God in a tough spot. He either has to protect everybody equally or not at all. So either nobody ever has anything bad happen to them, everybody has things bad happen to them exactly equally, or the good and the bad get spread around unevenly according to what we might call the "clumping principle," since the universe clumps, so do troubles clump, some people getting more, some less, more troubles happening to us in clumps rather than evenly spread throughout our lives at predictable intervals. Troubles and tragedies clump, too, just like everything else in the universe.

If we are (as I and many others are) as concerned about the suffering that is experienced by millions and billions around the planet because of disease, war, genocides, famines, plagues, poverty, bad water, lack of food, lack of opportunity, lack of access to justice, living under oppressive and immoral governments, and so on, and if we are upset with God over his seeming lack of concern, and we say "God, a loving God would stop those evil things and evil people and protect the innocent—why don't you stop the evil?" then, if we stop to think, we find ourselves with a different problem, one that we share with pretty much everyone. We want God to stop the evil *way over there*, but we don't want him to interfere with the evil we ourselves commit. We want him to have stopped Hitler, Stalin and Mao, to stop genocide in Darfur and war in the Middle East, to stop AIDS in Africa and polio in Pittsburgh, but we don't want him to stop, say, me. I want my freedom maintained, but I want him to take away, ultimately, everybody else's freedom to choose, as the circle of my concern tightens until it just includes, say, me, and the universe of my indifference expands to include everything that isn't, say, me.

We are all sociopaths. We are all Job. It's a little silly, really.

And God's answer to us is, "It's your job to stop evil and ameliorate suffering, not mine. As I made you the observers, unique among all creatures, so have I given you the task of helping those who need help. See 'the Good Samaritan' if you're confused about what that means."

(Parenthetical question: Why does it matter to help? It won't change anything.

It matters because God tells us to do it. It matters because if it's important to God, and if God is important to us, then it should matter to us. It's important because it involves us with God in redeeming the world, in the battle against evil and suffering, because it magnifies and intensifies our relationship with God, because the results of what we try to do in helping are magnified by God. It matters because in trying to be the Fractal Jesus, we are setting out to do his work and his will, to live out his salvation that rests within us, that we are not just saved to be saved from sin and condemnation, but we are saved to manifest the power of his salvation to the world around us. Christ helped others, healed, raised, forgave others not just to heal and raise and forgive them, but to demonstrate his living presence as the Fractal Jesus within us, to lead others into that presence, and ultimately to build God's kingdom on earth.)

It is ultimately not just God's existence that matters, because if he existed but had no concern for us and his creation, then so what? A God who does not care is irrelevant.

The problem then lies with a God who cares for us. If he cares, then why doesn't he care for us in the open and obvious ways that he ought to care for us, by protecting us from evil?

And the answer to that question comes again in the person of Christ. It is Jesus who by his very existence demonstrates how deep and wide and long is the love of God for us, and who also shows, by the fact that God did not protect him from suffering, that God's relationship with us is not defined by our comfort level.

The evil and suffering that afflicts us all inside our Black Hole of Indifference reminds us painfully that we are not God, that we are not in control, and that we need God to be with us, to come alongside us when we suffer, because God is deeply and intimately involved with us through Christ and the Holy Spirit. It also is meant to remind us that evil and suffering are not just for others in far distant lands where we have transient and occasional concern for them, but for us, and in so doing, reminds us that God is not just for us, but also for them, and that he is also a God who is in the far and distant places, with the far and distant peoples. He is not just my God for my needs and my salvation, but the God of creation who is for all peoples in all times and for the salvation of all.

So now we have a universe created by God with some mysterious, unknowable purpose in mind that is so all-fired important that it is worth all of this suffering, and let's not delude ourselves: there is a vast, almost endless sea of appalling, inconceivable suffering that has sewaged over humanity since its arrival in the cosmos, much of it done by humans to humans, but a lot of it done by nature to humans.

The scientific evidence is strong that God as creator exists. The evidence is strong that the universe was created to produce humans, because there was a path the universe seemed to take from Big Bang to Bob's Big Boy. Free will and choice are central to our existence, and therefore central to the purpose of the universe.

But although free will is responsible for many of the evil acts of history, man to man, still it is possible for a comet to fall on your head, a volcano to bury your village, a tsunami to sweep away 250,000 people into the sea, an earthquake to bury tens or hundreds of thousands of sleeping people under mountains of rubble, a drought to send millions into famine and hence into death, a monsoon to flood the homes of millions, and the list goes on, none of these due to free will but simply to the whims of nature.

The really aggravating part to the story is that we can't even call any of these things evil or even tragic without having a supreme being around to give those terms meaning. So God, ultimately the apparent cause of it all, can't be blamed, because he made the rules and gave us the morals and ethics that we would want to use to complain about the rules and the morals and the ethics and ultimately about God himself.

My only real choice is to be mad at God for not living up to his own standards, while I'm not doing a good job at living up to my own standards, much less his. God, you're doing a lousy job at being God, and I know I'm doing a lousy job of being me and don't have the right really to be pointing fingers, but I think you are doing a much worse job at being God than I am at being me, frankly. Even though the only reason I can say that is by using your rules, so I'm basically screwed. But, really, can't you just do a better job at being God?

And who gets to define what doing a "better job at being God" gets to be? Right. God. Not me. Nuts.

If you think I like the direction this is heading, you're crazy.

Maybe we need a new paradigm.

A New Paradigm: Let's start at the beginning. The traditional view of creation is to take Genesis 1-3 as being an accurate, scientific representation of creation, and perhaps it is, but not in the way that we have understood it to be. So let's consider it.

First, let's say that the Bible is true, even if we're not always quite sure what that means. We each have bits of scripture that don't make sense to us, and we always have.

If you go back to your birth, infancy and childhood as a Christian, no matter how old you were as a human at the time, the Bible was brand new and very cool, but immensely confusing. As time went on, you studied, listened to people who knew lots more than you did, read a lot, prayed a lot, and began to understand the difficult parts better. We are much more mature in our understanding of scripture than we used to be. As Mark Twain wrote, it's not the parts of the Bible that I *don't* understand that are the problem.

But (this is key), none of us are there yet, and we each tend to have our own understandings that we favor. That's why we have so many denominations. Each one has its own learned interpretation of the Bible. Everybody thinks his or her interpretation is correct, and that everybody else is wrong.

Part 1 of the New Paradigm: Everybody is wrong somewhere critical, somewhere that really matters. Each denomination believes something that is really, really wrong. Something that really, really matters. And what's more, each one of us as believers has something that we are really, really wrong about, something that really, really matters. If I were to point it out to you, you wouldn't agree, you'd get upset, you might call me a heretic, and you might burn me at the stake or throw me out of heaven, but it's true, nonetheless. We are all getting better (we hope) in understanding what the Bible says, but we will never be finished on that journey. None of us. Nobody. So have some grace. It's a useful thing to keep around just in case you might be wrong about something.

I could be wrong about this, but I don't think so. See, case in point.

Part 2: God is (in case you missed it so far) complicated, way too complicated for us to understand except through the example he gave us in Christ, and Jesus is complicated, too, way too complicated for us to understand. God will never fit into any box of understanding we care to build around him, but we each have a box that we think God, and Jesus, fit into. They don't.

Your box is too small. Mine is bigger than yours, probably, but it's still too small. If it's a box, it's too small. And the places where God and Jesus don't fit aren't the liberal or conservative places that you might think they are, because those are the places where you just disagree with someone else's interpretation of the whole thing. The places where they don't fit are the things you don't know about at all.

Part 3: The universe is (in case you missed it so far) complicated, way too complicated for us to understand, but just like we are getting better at understanding the Bible, God, and Jesus, we are getting better at understanding nature. We're not there yet, and I predict that we will never get it all, but we understand a lot of what makes the universe tick. We each have a box that we put our understanding of the universe into, and we think it fits.

It doesn't. Your box is too small. Mine is bigger than yours, probably, but it's still too small. If it's a box, it's too small. And the places where nature and the universe don't fit aren't the creationist or evolutionist places that you might think they are, because those are the places where you just disagree with someone else's science of the whole thing. The places where they don't fit are the things you don't know about at all. Whoa. Déjà vu.

Part 4: If God created the universe, then it is not an unreasonable assumption to make that in our studies of both God and the universe, our understandings of both will be enriched by our understanding of the other. Whereas current scientists want to say that science and religion are, to use Gould's terminology, "separate magisteria,"[122] entirely unrelated, each incapable of offering any insight about the other, science not able to offer evidence for God's existence, religion incapable of saying anything accurate or meaningful about nature, if God did create the universe and all the science that drives it, then as time

---

[122] Stephen Jay Gould, *Rocks of Ages*

passes, what we understand about God and what we understand about science will come increasingly closer together.

This is not to say, you might note, that science will come closer to religion, as though religion has it all right and science is all wrong, but that both will come closer to some distant truth about which we know something, but not everything about creation and its creator.

Evidence? As we have shown, religion once believed in a geocentric universe and a flat earth. Science once believed in an infinite universe in time and space. Both were wrong, and neither one liked being wrong. Many religious people still believe in a 6000-year-old universe. Most scientists still believe in an entirely and absolutely reductionist universe. We are on a continuum of progress, the progress shown by the fact that both science and religion now believe in a universe that had a starting point, possibly the most radical physical and metaphysical shift in human history.

Astronomer Robert Jastrow once famously wrote that "for the scientist who has lived by his faith in the power of reason, the story ends like a bad dream. He's scaled the mountains of ignorance. He's about to conquer the highest peak. As he pulls himself over the final rock, he is greeted by a band of theologians who have been sitting there for centuries."[123] Religious people tend to chortle when they hear the quote.

But the corollary truth may be that we will end up reading, "For the believer who has lived by his faith in the power of God, the story ends like a bad dream. He's scaled the mountains of unbelief. He's about to conquer the highest peak of skepticism. As he pulls himself over the final rock, he is greeted by a band of scientists who have been sitting there for about five minutes."

If God is the creator, then the patterns and mathematics of nature are his creation, and both science and religion will experience, as Indiana Jones' father (Mr. Jones, or "Dad") once said, "illumination."

Let us pursue a new paradigm of illumination. We have laid much of the foundation. So let's talk about life.

God had created a universe that was compelled to produce intelligent life. He created a universe with rules; to remind ourselves, let's hear again from Eugene Wigner: "The enormous usefulness of mathematics in the natural sciences is something bordering on the mysterious and . . . there is no rational explanation for it," and from Richard Feynman, "Why nature is mathematical is a mystery. . . . The fact that there are rules at all is a kind of miracle."

From the beginning, the rules are what caused everything to happen. This was God's design, but it does not seem to be a design that came with blueprints

---

[123] Robert Jastrow, *God and the Astronomers*

aimed at a specific structure at the end of the game. Rather, the universe and its rules were in turn ruled by what we are calling Complexity Theory, that sliver child of Chaos that provides the universe with the self-organizing capacity to leap gaping chasms into vastly more complex systems on a deliberate path to produce intelligent life.

Here it is that both science and religion will need to swallow hard and reconsider deeply held beliefs. It may be that there is an evolutionary process that took simple life to complex life, eventually to intelligent, self-aware, sentient life, and we in the religious community may need to admit to this process as being part of God's plan.

But the evolutionary community will need to abandon concepts which it has regarded as key: random mutation, natural selection, and gradualism may need to be set gently aside as the real mechanism for evolutionary change comes to the forefront of the theory. Part of the theory as it now stands is that there is no goal other than survival, no direction nor any directedness to evolutionary processes.

Is evolution operating in the biosphere? Clearly. But those processes are not primarily driven by random mutations that accidentally provide for better survivability in the face of some environmental change. There is too much evidence throughout the biosphere of organisms and systems of organisms responding with intent and specificity to environmental change; not perfectly, not always, and not always successfully, but that is the essence of Chaos—unpredictability—that gives the universe, the earth, and humanity the glorious richness that makes it all so fascinating.

There is even a hint from within the evolutionary community itself that these deliberate, intentional, specific responses to changes in the environment can change the genetic code, rather than vice versa, a theory that was rejected long ago but which has now returned. It may not be random, gradual change at the genetic level that ensures survival, but intentional, sudden, directed change that provides for survival, and then rewrites the code for future generations to benefit from. Complexity Theory begins to give us the tools to describe this process of sudden, unpredictable, creative, often non-perfect leaps in complexity, part of the natural compulsion to order as the universe has been programmed to pursue. Seeking after higher order is what the universe does, and is designed to do.

There is only one goal—for intelligent beings to arrive in the universe to interact with the universe, with each other, and with God. There is not, nor has there ever been, a pure and perfect path designed from Big Bang to Tiny Tim. It has always been a chaotic, unpredictable path, a fractal path with deep levels of creativity and beauty driven by deceptively simple rules of math and physics, those beautifully simple rules that physicists have discovered in part and which they long to find in full. There have been dead ends, extinctions, biopic explosions, false starts, all with the ultimate and inevitable goal in mind, but never with a specific path to follow. Were all of earth's plants and creatures designed? None were. All emerged from the simple rules that ordered the universe as life responded to need. It is all emergent, not designed. The only thing that was designed was the rules.

God made science at the beginning, science and the potential for science to emerge into the universe to take it on its intended path. Everything emerged from the interactions between particles and forces; it is all emergent. Although it is possible for God to have made an entire universe via miraculous acts, everything springing into being over a six-day period, to accept this story at face value is to say that the rules that organize nature came afterward, almost as an afterthought, as though there was a moment when he flipped a switch and the laws of nature came on like light into a room full of created things.

We might prefer to think that the rules came first with the intent to produce order, and that created things emerged from the process as science now generally describes it. Fundamental forces, particles, interactions, atomic nuclei, atoms, gas, clouds, stars, chemicals, planets, and life.

Life then would be emergent, inevitable. We may never know how life arrived, but its arrival was an inevitable part of the process of producing, ultimately, humans, and so there must be a natural explanation for the arrival of life. In saying that, we must recognize that every leap of complexity is, on the face of it, unlikely and unpredictable, the outcome unknowable and indescribable. But when winding the clock backwards, we sometimes can describe how it must have happened if we make the right assumptions about the way our non-random, non-accidental universe works.

The leap from non-life to life, from inanimate chemicals to animate biology, from dust to living things was extraordinary: there was no way that it could have been predicted or foreknown by anything that might have been there to foreknow it (which would have been living, so that goes without saying), and when it happened, it would have been breathtaking, so unexpected as to boggle any mind which of course could not have been there, or any mind which now is here to wonder about it.

And yet, in its unpredictability, its unknowability, its stunning unexpectedness, it was still built into the fabric of existence. It was the next step on the path toward intelligence. Though unbelievably unlikely, it was absolutely necessary and inevitable.

Was the intent of the universe then to produce humans? Even though we've said it directly, the answer is, no. The intent of the universe was to produce sentient, self-aware, intelligent beings whose scientific *raison d'etre* was to interact with the universe and cause reality to come into being, and whose religious *raison d'etre* was to interact with each other, with the creation and its creatures, and with the creator. It was to bring out of free will, relationship and love into the cosmos. Humans were the answer, though probably not specifically and physically the goal as we now exist.

So does everything look like God intended for it to look? Truthfully, I have no idea how God intended for anything to look, but if the rules give us any clue, then he set the universe with its rules freely on its path toward complex organisms and sentience with no plan for physical appearance for anything in the universe at all—not stars, galaxies, planets, moons, night skies over deserts, kudus or pudus, gnus or emus, wildebeests or Tasmanian devils, sumo wrestlers, ballerinas, you, me, or anybody or anything else. I'm guessing he had no plan for ears, eyes, toes, legs, knees, feet, arms, heads, hair, bunions, corns, pimples, baldness, spleens, or any other part of anybody's body anywhere.

I'm guessing he had a plan for creatures who could love and be loved, who could worship or reject him, and what they looked like was pretty immaterial.

He gave the universe simple rules, $y=z^2+c$, $e=mc^2$, $G_{\mu\nu}=8\pi T_{\mu\nu}$, for example, and from these elegant, beautiful, stunning, powerful rules, starting from a single dimensionless point of pure energy potential, he set the universe on its path toward phenomenal complexity and hence to sentience, chaos out of order, order out of chaos. From simple origins, amazingly complex results, and the only word that fits it all is, beautiful.

It has all emerged, but not like the Creature from the Black Lagoon, some random monster that is what it is by accident. It has emerged from the beauty of the math and the physics according to the way God planned for it to be, but not a plan like we might expect, in our limited focus and understanding, but a plan with both structure and unpredictability, with rules that would give the result the plan was designed to produce, but not within a tight construct, a narrow range of possibilities, but a broad, sweeping, cosmic near-infinity of gorgeousness.

Conclusion

The End

The End? Really? I don't think so.

First, I can't violate my own observations by assuming that science the way that it's been presented here is finished, or even right. It's correct now, within limits, but in a day, a week, a month, a year, a thousand years, everything can and probably will change. We'll make new discoveries. We may find evidence for the multiverse, or for multiple Big Bangs, or for five-dimensional Membranes lurking a proton's length from the end of our noses that occasionally and randomly touch to produce Big Bangs and universes, or for String Theory, or for Loop Quantum Gravity, or for things that we haven't even thought of yet. We may discover that Big Bang isn't true, or that the forces of nature have varied in their strengths over time.

We may find a way for the universe to be ordered that needs no orderer, though I myself can't imagine how, or that our understanding (or lack of it) of the quantum is wrong and the need for observers vanishes like a virtual particle, the baffling foundation of nature's structure once again reasonable and non-weird.

We may discover that everything we thought we knew about nature is wrong. It's happened before. What's to prevent it from happening again? We are limited by the strength, power, and subtlety of our ability to make observations, and there are clear limits to those abilities, limits imposed by time, space, energy, and size. We may overcome those limits, we may not.

Will we then take what we know at that moment and use it to endorse God's existence, or to deny it? Probably. Will we do so credibly? Many, with short memories, will think so. Should science and religion keep their distance, *separate magisteria* after all? I don't think it likely, but people like me have been radically wrong more than once.

Second, am I happy now with God on the issue of suffering, that which I have defined as being one of the two defining issues of faith faced by humanity? No, not especially. You and I have been given hearts for compassion and love, and those hearts, which are the end point of creation, can never be satisfied with any explanation for suffering. If I had just stayed in my own sociopathic Black Hole of Concern, worried about my tiny circle of friends and family, or maybe, safer still, just concerned about my own $(HW)^2$, then theoretically I could be content with the arrangement, because I wouldn't care about the suffering that humanity has inflicted upon itself, and that it has experienced courtesy of Mother Nature.

I say "theoretically" because, of course, the smaller my Black Hole of Concern, the more dissatisfied I would be with any slight level of discomfort or displeasure, so I would really be much less satisfied with the arrangements, only from a purely narcissistic point of view that would generate no sympathy from anyone else on any terms. But at least at that point, everyone else could say, "See, that's why the world sucks. It's because of guys like him!"

But I have seen and touched desperate poverty in the slums of Watts, Nairobi, Johannesburg, Manila, Phnom Penh, Lima, Quito, Hanoi, Hong Kong, Shanghai, Tashkent, Saigon, and Kampala. I have worked and lived in the indifferent wealth of Beverly Hills, Pebble Beach, Zurich and Geneva, and have seen the indifferent wealth of Santiago, Mexico City, Nairobi, and Johannesburg. I know some who have fled oppression, child soldiery, refugee camps, and invasions. I have seen and read too much of child slavery and prostitution, of torture, abuse, rape, and violence, knowing as you know of the horror of tsunamis, genocides, serial killings, slaughter, earthquakes, hurricanes, floods, airplane crashes, pointless wars (as though there are wars that have a point).

I know, as you know, of these stories, and I cannot imagine how a God of love can stand by and watch when the slightest touch, the tiniest breath or whisper, the most miniscule of delays or accelerations would have changed lives beyond imagining. Surely a Ted Bundy or a Henry Lucas could have been caught before the hundreds or thousands of innocent lives were lost to kidnapping, rape, torture, and slow, excruciating death. Surely a Hitler or a Pol Pot could have stepped in front of a bus one day. Surely the bullets could have missed Martin Luther King, Jr. or John Kennedy, just as surely as they could have hit Stalin or Mao. Surely a Quantum, Chaotic God can Look the Look or nudge the Butterfly and change things just enough in just the right way.

And perhaps he does, and we never know about it. But there are levels of horror that I cannot imagine ignoring, if I were God.

But God is God, and I am not. I wrote a little tune for David's psalm once:

> My heart is not proud, O Lord, my eyes are not haughty; I do not concern myself with great matters or things too wonderful for me. But I have stilled and quieted my soul; like a weaned child with its mother, like a weaned child is my soul within me. O Israel, put your hope in the Lord both now and forevermore.[124]

---

[124] Psalm 131: 1-3 (NIV)

I wrote it to remind myself that I don't believe it, and should. I absolutely *do* concern myself with great matters and with things too wonderful for me, and I have not yet begun to still or quiet my soul. And so I must have a proud heart and haughty eyes, and I wonder if I put my hope in the Lord at all.

But I know that God wants anything but indifference from us toward the horrors of the world around us. He wants our hearts to be stressed and sore. He wants our anger and frustration. But he only wants it if that anger and frustration causes us to get up from the pile of ashes, throw aside the bit of pottery we use to scrape our own sores, and go off to try to fix what is wrong with the world. We will not fix it for everyone. But we may fix it for some.

Third, in so doing, we will solve the second great problem and question of life: does it have any meaning and purpose? Is there a reason why I am here, a reason for my existence? Why am I here?

I have begun to suspect that the two great problems of existence, suffering and meaning, are not isolated questions, but intimately related. They cannot be solved in isolation, but must be solved together in a fractalated, relational sort of way. The nugget of wisdom in the story of the Good Samaritan is this: the religious people who were too busy to stop and help were condemned in the story. Religion is not the answer.

Allow me to suggest that we could rewrite the story to cause two *scientists* to hurry by the hurt and dying man, ignoring him because they were focused, as the religious people were, on "great matters" and "things too wonderful." Knowledge is not the answer.

It was the man who stopped, angry at the suffering that he saw around him all the time as he walked on the roads, at people hanging in agony on crosses, rejected and shunned as lepers, blind or lame and reduced to begging, orphaned or widowed and thrown out of society, minorities, as he himself was a rejected and shunned minority, denied equal protection and opportunity in society, the poor, the homeless, the immigrant, the foreigner, the victims of disease or fire or war or famine or plague or flooding or drought or earthquakes or hurricanes or tsunamis or rapists or killers or robbers, all of them cast aside into the ditch to die as the rest of the decent world walked by without a glance or a care, each wrapped up in his or her Black Hole of Concern. It was this man, angry at God and man and nature, who stopped, and picked him up, cleaned him, cared for him, put him in a safe place; it was this man whom Jesus singled out and praised. He was the Fractal Jesus, the little bit of love that becomes an entire universe of love expressed in a tiny, forgettable, ignored act of apparently pointless charity.

Here's what Jesus said:

> "When the Son of Man comes in his glory, and all the angels with him, he will sit on his throne in heavenly glory. All the nations will be gathered before him, and he will separate the people one from another as a shepherd separates the sheep from the goats. He will put the sheep on his right and the goats on his left.
>
> "Then the King will say to those on his right, 'Come, you who are blessed by my Father; take your inheritance, the kingdom prepared for you since the creation of the world. For I was hungry and you gave me something to eat, I was thirsty and you gave me something to drink, I was a stranger and you invited me in, I needed clothes and you clothed me, I was sick and you looked after me, I was in prison and you came to visit me.'
>
> "Then the righteous will answer him, 'Lord, when did we see you hungry and feed you, or thirsty and give you something to drink? When did we see you a stranger and invite you in, or needing clothes and clothe you? When did we see you sick or in prison and go to visit you?'
>
> "The King will reply, 'I tell you the truth, whatever you did for one of the least of these brothers of mine, you did for me.'
>
> "Then he will say to those on his left, 'Depart from me, you who are cursed, into the eternal fire prepared for the devil and his angels. For I was hungry and you gave me nothing to eat, I was thirsty and you gave me nothing to drink, I was a stranger and you did not invite me in, I needed clothes and you did not clothe me, I was sick and in prison and you did not look after me.'
>
> "They also will answer, 'Lord, when did we see you hungry or thirsty or a stranger or needing clothes or sick or in prison, and did not help you?'
>
> "He will reply, 'I tell you the truth, whatever you did not do for one of the least of these, you did not do for me.'
>
> "Then they will go away to eternal punishment, but the righteous to eternal life."[125]

That's not religion. That's the meaning to life. That's why you're here.

You've got a choice—the sociopathic Black Hole of Self-Absorption and the Expanding Universe of Massive Indifference, or the Fractal Jesus.

Your call.

---

[125] Matt 25:31-46 (NIV)

Extra Bits

Articles providing current evidence for free will, a universe that ultimately cannot be understood, and new limitations on natural selection and random mutation:

Does Free Will exist?

Free will not an illusion after all – New Scientist Magazine

Champions of free will take heart. A landmark 1980s experiment that purported to show free will doesn't exist is being challenged.

In 1983, neuroscientist Benjamin Libet asked volunteers wearing scalp electrodes to flex a finger or wrist. When they did, the movements were preceded by a dip in the signals being recorded, called the "readiness potential". Libet interpreted this RP as the brain preparing for movement.

Crucially, the RP came a few tenths of a second before the volunteers said they had decided to move. Libet concluded that unconscious neural processes determine our actions before we are ever aware of making a decision (*Brain*, vol 106, p 623).

Since then, others have quoted the experiment as evidence that free will is an illusion - a conclusion that was always controversial, particularly as there is no proof the RP represents a decision to move.

Long sceptical of Libet's interpretation, Jeff Miller and Judy Trevena of the University of Otago in Dunedin, New Zealand, attempted to tease apart what prompts the RP using a similar experiment, with a key twist.

They also used scalp electrodes, but instead of letting their volunteers decide when to move, Miller and Trevena asked them to wait for an audio tone before deciding whether to tap a key. If Libet's interpretation were correct, Miller reasoned, the RP should be greater after the tone when a person chose to tap the key.

While there was an RP before volunteers made their decision to move, the signal was the same whether or not they elected to tap. Miller concludes that the RP may merely be a sign that the brain is paying attention and does not indicate that a decision has been made (*Consciousness and Cognition*, DOI: 10.1016/j.concog.2009.08.006).

Miller and Trevena also failed to find evidence of subconscious decision-making in a second experiment. This time they asked volunteers to press a key after the tone, but to decide on the spot whether to use their left or right hand. As movement in the right limbs is related to the brain signals in the left hemisphere and vice versa, they reasoned that if an unconscious process is driving this decision, where it occurs in the brain should depend on which hand is chosen. But they found no such correlation.

Marcel Brass of Ghent University in Belgium says it is wrong to use Miller and Trevena's results to reinterpret Libet's experiment, in which volunteers were not prompted to make a decision. The audio tone "changes the paradigm", so the two can't be compared, he says. What's more, in 2008, he and his colleagues detected patterns in brain activity that predicted better than chance whether or not a subject would press a key, before they were aware of making a decision (*Nature Neuroscience*, DOI: 10.1038/nn.2112).

But Frank Durgin, a psychologist at Swarthmore College in Pennsylvania, says that Brass's results do "seem to undermine Libet's preferred interpretation", though they don't contradict it outright.

www.newscientist.com/article/mg20327274.400-free-will-not-an-illusion-after-all.html

Can we ultimately know everything about the universe?

A mathematical theory places limits on how much a physical entity can know about the past, present or future

By Graham P. Collins, Scientific American Magazine

Deep in the deluge of knowledge that poured forth from science in the 20th century were found ironclad limits on what we can know. Werner Heisenberg discovered that improved precision regarding, say, an object's position inevitably degraded the level of certainty of its momentum. Kurt Gödel showed that within any formal mathematical system advanced enough to be useful, it is impossible to use the system to prove every true statement that it contains. And Alan Turing demonstrated that one cannot, in general, determine if a computer algorithm is going to halt.

David H. Wolpert, a physics-trained computer scientist at the NASA Ames Research Center, has chimed in with his version of a knowledge limit. Because of it, he concludes, the universe lies beyond the grasp of any intellect, no matter how powerful, that could exist within the universe. Specifically, during the past two years, he has been refining a proof that no matter what laws of physics govern a universe, there are inevitably facts about the universe that its inhabitants cannot learn by experiment or predict with a computation. Philippe M. Binder, a physicist at the University of Hawaii at Hilo, suggests that the theory implies researchers seeking unified laws cannot hope for anything better than a "theory of almost everything."

Wolpert's work is an effort to create a formal rigorous description of processes such as measuring a quantity, observing a phenomenon, predicting a system's future state or remembering past information—a description that is general enough to be independent of the laws of physics. He observes that all those processes share a common basic structure: something must be configured (whether it be an experimental apparatus or a computer to run a simulation); a question about the universe must be specified; and an answer (right or wrong) must be supplied. He models that general structure by defining a class of mathematical entities that he calls inference devices.

The inference devices act on a set of possible universes. For instance, our universe, meaning the entire world line of our universe over all time and space, could be a member of the set of all possible such universes permitted by the same rules that govern ours. Nothing needs to be specified about those rules in Wolpert's analysis. All that matters is that the various possible inference devices supply answers to questions in each universe. In a universe similar to ours, an inference device may involve a set of digital scales that you will stand on at noon tomorrow and the question relate to your mass at that time. People may also be inference devices or parts of one.

Wolpert proves that in any such system of universes, quantities exist that cannot be ascertained by any inference device inside the system. Thus, the "demon" hypothesized by Pierre-Simon Laplace in the early 1800s (give the demon the exact positions and velocities of every particle in the universe, and it will compute the future state of the universe) is stymied if the demon must be a part of the universe.

Researchers have proved results about the incomputability of specific physical systems before. Wolpert points out that his result is far more general, in that it makes virtually no assumptions about the laws of physics and it requires no limits on the computational power of the inference device other than it must exist within the universe in question. In addition, the result applies not only to predictions of a physical system's future state but also to observations of a present state and examining a record of a past state.

The theorem's proof, similar to the results of Gödel's incompleteness theorem and Turing's halting problem, relies on a variant of the liar's paradox—ask Laplace's demon to predict the following yes/no fact about the future state of the universe: "Will the universe not be one in which your answer to this question is yes?" For the demon, seeking a true yes/no answer is like trying to determine the truth of "This statement is false." Knowing the exact current state of the entire universe, knowing all the laws governing the universe and having unlimited computing power is no help to the demon in saying truthfully what its answer will be.

In a sense, however, the existence of such a paradox is not exactly earth-shattering. As Scott Aaronson, a computer scientist at the Massachusetts Institute of Technology, puts it: "That your predictions about the universe are fundamentally constrained by you yourself being part of the universe you're predicting, always seemed pretty obvious to me—and I doubt Laplace himself would say otherwise if we could ask him." Aaronson does allow, though, that it is "often a useful exercise to spell out all the assumptions behind an idea, recast everything in formal notation and think through the implications in detail," as Wolpert has done. After all, the devil, or demon, is in the details.

The Standard Model of neo-Darwinian Evolutionary Theory – random mutation and natural selection are the engines that drive evolution. True?

Geography And History Shape Genetic Differences In Humans – from Science Daily, 7 June 2009

New research indicates that natural selection may shape the human genome much more slowly than previously thought. Other factors -- the movements of humans within and among continents, the expansions and contractions of populations, and the vagaries of genetic chance – have heavily influenced the distribution of genetic variations in populations around the world.

In recent years, geneticists have identified a handful of genes that have helped human populations adapt to new environments within just a few thousand years—a strikingly short timescale in evolutionary terms. However, the team found that for most genes, it can take at least 50,000-100,000 years for natural selection to spread favorable traits through a human population. According to their analysis, gene variants tend to be distributed throughout the world in patterns that reflect ancient population movements and other aspects of population history.

"We don't think that selection has been strong enough to completely fine-tune the adaptation of individual human populations to their local environments," says co-author Jonathan Pritchard. "In addition to selection, demographic history -- how populations have moved around -- has exerted a strong effect on the distribution of variants."

To determine whether the frequency of a particular variant resulted from natural selection, Pritchard and his colleagues compared the distribution of variants in parts of the genome that affect the structure and regulation of proteins to the distribution of variants in parts of the genome that do not affect proteins. Since these neutral parts of the genome are less likely to be affected by natural selection, they reasoned that studying variants in these regions should reflect the demographic history of populations.

The researchers found that many previously identified genetic signals of selection may have been created by historical and demographic factors rather than by selection. When the team compared closely related populations they found few large genetic differences. If the individual populations' environments were exerting strong selective pressure, such differences should have been apparent.

Selection may still be occurring in many regions of the genome, says Pritchard. But if so, it is exerting a moderate effect on many genes that together influence a biological characteristic. "We don't know enough yet about the genetics of most human traits to be able to pick out all of the relevant variation," says Pritchard. "As functional studies go forward, people will start figuring out the phenotypes that are associated with selective signals," says lead author Graham Coop. "That will be very important, because then we can figure out what selection pressures underlie these episodes of natural selection."

But even with further research, much will remain unknown about the processes that have resulted in human traits. In particular, Pritchard and Coop urge great caution in trying to link selection with complex characteristics like intelligence. "We're in the infancy of trying to understand what signals of selection are telling us," says Coop, "so it's a very long jump to attribute cultural features and group characteristics to selection."

www.sciencedaily.com/releases/2009/06/090605091157.htm

Epigenetics: 100 Reasons To Change The Way We Think About Genetics – from Science Daily 20 May 2009

For years, genes have been considered the one and only way biological traits could be passed down through generations of organisms.

Not anymore.

Increasingly, biologists are finding that non-genetic variation acquired during the life of an organism can sometimes be passed on to offspring—a phenomenon known as epigenetic inheritance. An article forthcoming in the July issue of *The Quarterly Review of Biology* lists over 100 well-documented cases of epigenetic inheritance between generations of organisms, and suggests that non-DNA inheritance happens much more often than scientists previously thought.

Biologists have suspected for years that some kind of epigenetic inheritance occurs at the cellular level. The different kinds of cells in our bodies provide an example. Skin cells and brain cells have different forms and functions, despite having exactly the same

DNA. There must be mechanisms—other than DNA—that make sure skin cells stay skin cells when they divide.

Only recently, however, have researchers begun to find molecular evidence of non-DNA inheritance between organisms as well as between cells. The main question now is: How often does it happen?

"The analysis of these data shows that epigenetic inheritance is ubiquitous ...," write Eva Jablonka and Gal Raz, both of Tel-Aviv University in Israel. Their article outlines inherited epigenetic variation in bacteria, protists, fungi, plants, and animals.

These findings "represent the tip of a very large iceberg," the authors say.

For example, Jablonka and Raz cite a study finding that when fruit flies are exposed to certain chemicals, at least 13 generations of their descendants are born with bristly outgrowths on their eyes. Another study found that exposing a pregnant rat to a chemical that alters reproductive hormones leads to generations of sick offspring. Yet another study shows higher rates of heart disease and diabetes in the children and grandchildren of people who were malnourished in adolescence.

In these cases, as well as the rest of the cases Jablonka and Raz cite, the source of the variation in subsequent generations was not DNA. Rather, the new traits were carried on through epigenetic means.

There are four known mechanisms for epigenetic inheritance. According to Jablonka and Raz, the best understood of these is "DNA methylation." Methyls, small chemical groups within cells, latch on to certain areas along the DNA strand. The methyls serve as a kind of switch that renders genes active or inactive.

By turning genes on and off, methyls can have a profound impact on the form and function of cells and organisms, without changing the underlying DNA. If the normal pattern of methyls is altered—by a chemical agent, for example—that new pattern can be passed to future generations.

The result, as in the case of the pregnant rats, can be dramatic and stick around for generations, despite the fact that underlying DNA remains unchanged.

Lamarck revisited

New evidence for epigenetic inheritance has profound implications for the study of evolution, Jablonka and Raz say.

"Incorporating epigenetic inheritance into evolutionary theory extends the scope of evolutionary thinking and leads to notions of heredity and evolution that incorporate development," they write.

This is a vindication of sorts for 18th century naturalist Jean Baptiste Lamarck. Lamarck, whose writings on evolution predated Charles Darwin's, believed that evolution was driven in part by the inheritance of acquired traits. His classic example was the giraffe. Giraffe ancestors, Lamarck surmised, reached with their necks to munch leaves high in trees. The reaching caused their necks to become slightly longer— a trait that was passed on to descendants. Generation after generation inherited slightly longer necks, and the result is what we see in giraffes today.

With the advent of Mendelian genetics and the later discovery of DNA, Lamarck's ideas fell out of favor entirely. Research on epigenetics, while yet to uncover anything as dramatic as Lamarck's giraffes, does suggest that acquired traits can be heritable, and that Lamarck was not so wrong after all.

www.sciencedaily.com/releases/2009/05/090518111723.htm

Epigenetics: DNA Isn't Everything

April 13, 2009 — Research into epigenetics has shown that environmental factors affect characteristics of organisms. These changes are sometimes passed on to the offspring. Does this in any way oppose Darwin's theory ...

www.sciencedaily.com/releases/2009/04/090412081315.htm

Rethinking The Genetic Theory Of Inheritance: Heritability May Not Be Limited To DNA

January 20, 2009 — In the first study of its kind, scientists have detected evidence that DNA may not be the only carrier of heritable information; a secondary molecular mechanism called epigenetics may also account ...
www.sciencedaily.com/releases/2009/01/090118200632.htm

www.ingramcontent.com/pod-product-compliance
Lightning Source LLC
Chambersburg PA
CBHW032116090426
42743CB00007B/372